THE CALL TO HOSPITALITY

THE CALL TO HOSPITALITY

THE ORIGINS OF THE HOSPITALLER VOCATION

MARK TURNHAM ELVINS

GRACEWING

First published in England in 2013
by
Gracewing
2 Southern Avenue
Leominster
Herefordshire HR6 0QF
United Kingdom
www.gracewing.co.uk

No part of this publication may be reproduced, stored in a retrieval system, or transmitted in any form or by any means, electronic, mechanical, photocopying, recording or otherwise, without the written permission of the publisher.

The right of Mark Turnham Elvins to be identified as the author of this work has been asserted in accordance with the Copyright, Designs and Patents Act 1988.

© 2013 Mark Turnham Elvins

ISBN 978 085244 816 8

Typeset by Gracewing

Cover design by Bernardita Peña Hurtado

Cover painting: James Tissot, *Le pauvre Lazare à la porte du riche* (Poor Lazarus at the Rich Man's Door)
Date: between 1886 and 1894

Dedicated to the late Donald Lord Craigmyle
who had a great love for the poor,
to Michael Rapinet,
Nigel Stourton
and Peter Lloyd
whose tireless work has ensured the success
of the Orders of St John Care Trust.

Special thanks to David J. Critchley for his thorough editing of the text during the the illness of the author.

Contents

Foreword by Fra' Matthew Festing.....................xi

Introduction..xiii

1. The Good Action and Christian Fellowship............1

Fundamental Principles..................................3
    I. The Stranger....................................3
    II. Hospitality...................................4

2. 'Shelter the Homeless Poor': The Teaching of Scripture and its Application...........................9

3. Gospel Ethic..19

4. The Poor and the Writings of the Fathers............31

5. Monastic Hospitality................................43

6. Hospitals and Hospitallers..........................57

7. Our Lords the Poor..................................73

8. The Mediaeval Poor Law..............................81

9. Poor Relief in Mediaeval England....................89

10. The Dissolution and its Social Consequences in England..101

11. Post-Reformation Crisis in England................111

12. The Order of St John..............................117

13. The New Poor Law in England.......................125

14. The Re-Awakening of Christian Social Conscience in England....................................133

15. The Order of Malta and the Renaissance of
Hospitaller Work..139

Appendix...147

Bibliography..153
    Biblical Texts..153
    Primary Sources..153
    Secondary Sources.......................................155

In commemoration of the 900th anniversary of the founding of the Sovereign, Military, Hospitaller Order of St John of Jerusalem, Rhodes and Malta by the Bull of Pope Paschal II Pie Postulatio Voluntatis *in 1113.*

FOREWORD

IN THIS HIS latest book *The Call to Hospitality* Father Mark Elvins traces in a most interesting way the philosophy and teaching behind the Hospitaller movement throughout the world.

The teaching of the Church both in the Old and New Testaments together with the exhortations of the early Fathers of the Church are explained in a very readable fashion.

The author provides a fascinating account of the work of all the pre-Reformation Monastic Orders and of the Order of St John in particular. One of the many but often forgotten tragedies of the Reformation—the abandonment of so many poor pilgrims, wayfarers and displaced people—is movingly explained.

The development of the modern system of poor relief, particularly in the British Isles, is covered and brought right up-to-date in the context of current legislation and the Order of Malta's part in this work is interestingly explained.

I believe that this work will prove to be an influence of great interest for those who feel themselves ready to respond to *The Call to Hospitality*.

Fra' Matthew Festing
HMEH the Prince and Grand Master
of the Sovereign, Military and Hospitaller
Order of St John of Jerusalem, Rhodes and Malta.

Introduction

Hospitality to the poor is an idea fundamental to Christianity and was the most striking characteristic of the Church's ministry in ancient Rome. It was from the poor that many of the earliest Christians, described here by church historian Henri Daniel-Rops, were drawn:

> At first the Word had mainly affected very humble folk, the small wage-earners, all those fullers, cobblers, and wool-carders who had often been Christ's first witnesses and martyrs. It had proved the comforter of men of low degree, of people like Fortunatus, Achaicus, Urbanus, Hermas, Phlegon and Stephanus, all of whose names, clumsily carved upon their tombs in the catacombs, reveal their humble birth.[1]

This is hardly surprising as the early Christians in Rome shared their meagre benefits with all the poor who came to them. Despite persecution and the restrictions of life in the catacombs they gave food and shelter to the least of Christ's brethren. Thus when the recipients asked why they did them such a kindness they told them about the Lord Jesus. This was easily the most effective form of evangelism, the practice of the silent sermon of the evangelical virtues.

Bishops of the early Church were known as 'Fathers of the Poor' and by their consecration oath were bound to show 'mercy and kindness for the name of the Lord to the poor, the stranger and all in want.'[2] In the first century, Pope St Clement I explained to the Corinthians that those who give to the poor, give as to Christ;

in the third century the anonymous *Didascalia Apostolorum* listed the duties of a Christian towards the poor; in 370 St Basil the Great, bishop of Caesarea, built an entire village for the poor outside the city of Caesarea; and in the fifth century St Theodosius opened two hospitals for the poor near Jerusalem. In the sixth century, Pope St Gregory I recorded that a quarter of the Church's income was devoted to the poor,[3] while the Synod of Tours of 567 imposed on each parish the obligation of caring for the poor. The ninth century saw a revival under the reign of Charlemagne of the tradition that all Church property was the patrimony of the poor.

A new development occurred in Jerusalem in the late eleventh century when the community of St Mary of the Latins founded the Hospital of St John. By 1099 a lay brother called Gerard was the hospital's warden: he was apparently a Cassinese Benedictine who had broken ranks with his order. However Pope Paschal II's Bull *Pie Postulatio Voluntatis* of 1113 granted papal protection and special privileges to the new hospital and confirmed Gerard's status as its institutor. Gerard set new and radical standards, revealing a new spirit of philanthropy that stood in sharp contrast with what had gone before. He followed to the full the Gospel command to welcome all who came in need of food, drink, clothing and shelter as if they were Christ himself (Mt 25:34-40), thus creating a hospital which was a place of hospitality (cf. *domus hospitalis*) rather than an infirmary strictly for the sick, and which could welcome the poor and receive them with reverence and solicitude as if they were great lords.

Gerard's new order became known as the Hospitallers of St John of Jerusalem, and the Hospitallers now became the servants of the poor and the sick and served them as their lords. In this new radical interpretation of the Gospel, the Hospitallers served people of all faiths including Muslims and Jews, providing a hospitality that went straight to the heart of the Gospel. In addition to running its great hospital, the Order also pioneered the first field hospital and a maternity hospital and orphanage. Brothers and sisters could be found serving in the great hospital at Jerusalem: the brothers covering the administration and the sisters no doubt caring for the female inmates and helping in the kitchens. The employed staff also included physicians, barber surgeons, and male and female nurses. There was another hospital at Acre and at this early stage the members of the Order were strictly hospitaller and nothing more. The Order's contribution to the sick and the poor over the centuries has been second to none: they were the pioneers of having a bed for each patient with regular changes of bed linen and of using silver plate for purposes of hygiene. Their ideal of acting as servants of the sick and poor and of treating them as their lords proved a unique Gospel insight that has remained an inspiration to this day for all who aspire to the vocation of hospitality.

In pre-Reformation Britain the Church provided all the welfare, largely shelter and hospitality, for the sick and the poor. A roof and sustenance was the basic provision with a routine of prayers and daily Mass and a high standard of nursing. Medicine was primitive, but without the hospitality many would have perished by the wayside as they did when the religious hospitals were traded off in the Dissolution. From the Norman Conquest until the beginning of the sixteenth century the population in England did not exceed 4,000,000 and yet by the 1530s there were more than 750 religious hospitals or houses of hospitality, caring in the majority of cases for poor wayfarers, but also for the sick, the homeless, the aged, and orphans.

The monasteries, which numbered more than 1,500, likewise served the needs of the poor. The Benedictines usually maintained a hostel at the monastery gate, but the Augustinian brotherhoods became the champions of the poor in running religious hospitals, even if they never quite compared with the Hospitallers, who in declaring the poor to be their Lords, and in giving their Grand Master the title *Custos Pauperum,* or *Guardian of the Poor,* established a new kind of vocation.

Up until the Reformation in England it was possible for poor wayfarers to travel from parish to parish and find accommodation: there would seem to have been a culture of compassion. Even the sick had rest and attention in the religious hospitals, despite the inadequate medical provision, and all were supported by the prayers of the religious brethren. Some of these hospitals had become a bit run down by the sixteenth century, and had lost their zeal of the early middle ages, but nothing to justify their wholesale dissolution which swept aside a whole system of welfare and caused untold suffering.

The Elizabethan Poor Laws of 1572, 1597 and 1601 were no longer based on the motive of compassion on which the old mediaeval poor law had been based, and a kind of rigorous expediency lay behind the enforcement of the laws against so-called idle beggars. The first workhouse was established in Bristol in 1697, providing an incentive for other parishes to follow suit, and the Workhouse Test Act 1722-23 allowed every parish to provide such dwellings on condition that any

Introduction xvii

poor who refused to enter should forfeit any other relief whatsoever. This was a far cry from the generosity of the pre-Reformation religious houses. Poor relief had become a state charity funded by a tax on the ratepayer, providing only a penny-pinching relief.

The Relief of the Poor Act 1782 stipulated that the sick and infirm were to be sent to the workhouses, while the fit were to be given an allowance to enable them to labour on the land near their homes. The Removal Act 1795 was designed to prevent people from being removed to their place of birth so as not to be an expense on the rates, a practice which had sometimes not even allowed the poor to die in peace. Now no one could be forcibly removed until they had come onto the rates. The Poor Law Amendment Act 1834 provided relief for destitute wayfarers in the 'casual wards' of workhouses, but one Poor Law Commissioner was quoted as saying: 'Our object is to establish therein a discipline so severe and repulsive as to make them a terror to the poor and prevent them from entering.'[4]

In the 1940s Sir William Beveridge, an agnostic academic of the Liberal Party, sought to restore Christianity to politics by bringing back compassion in the care of the poor. This gave rise to the welfare state and the modern system of poor relief: yet despite all the sophistications of modern social work and all the benefits available to the impoverished, there is something to be learned from the days when the sick and the poor encountered Christian compassion and dedicated simplicity.

Notes

[1] H. Daniel-Rops, *The Church of Apostles and Martyrs*, trans. A. Butler (London & New York, J. M. Dent & Sons Ltd & E. P. Dutton & Co. Inc., 1960), pp. 200-201. See also pp. 333-334.
[2] See below, pp. 69–70.
[3] See below, p. 40.
[4] See below, p. 127.

CHAPTER 1

THE GOOD ACTION AND CHRISTIAN FELLOWSHIP

Is THE DESIRE to do good an isolated experience, without an author and without an end? Many want to do good to others whom they see to be in need, and yet cannot explain why, beyond a sense of solidarity with the sufferer. This altruistic urge often arises from a natural sympathy, or from a sense of what is right, without any frame of reference incorporating an ultimate goal, or any understanding of a source of inspiration. For some, doing good may initially be an isolated experience, but the pleasure it gives them compels them to further acts of charity, in order to renew the sense of purpose and usefulness that it gives to their existence.[1] Doing good can give meaning to the life of someone wanting to contribute positively to a world which is seemingly governed by caprice and where disaster, suffering, and death have no apparent explanation or redress. Utopianism has passed, there seems no brave new tomorrow and yet the brooding threat of annihilation seems to have enhanced the desire to improve the quality of life, while it lasts, and to extend the benefits of modern society to all, and particularly to the poor and the suffering. There appears to be a plentiful reservoir of good will and a desire to contribute to human need, evidenced by the phenomenal results of fund raising for the starving in North Africa, and by the dedicated physicians, nurses and scientists who labour to improve man's lot, and of course the ever increasing popularity of social work.

Some will act on Christian conviction or out of respect for Christian values, but the values that motivate others to altruism are very varied. The values of human worth, freedom, and fulfilment have at present a populist ascendancy and these imply a materialistic rather than a Christian scale of priorities. Thus in social studies the all-pervasive emphasis is on the here and now, on the transient condition of man and the search for some temporary good. Individual needs make up the whole human condition and creating a fairer and more just society is understandably of the utmost importance. So far as public life is concerned, however, this is a subjective view, arising from a school of thought, a party policy or an influential whim, according to the fancy of the day; what is needed is a universally respected frame of reference incorporating the ultimate good. Without an understanding of the ultimate good, the inevitable criterion for action is temporary expediency, so often the basis of modern law making, and laws framed on this basis are not only open to exploitation but can, with changed circumstances, even cause injustice. The immutable elements of the ultimate good, such as the sacredness of human life, were perceived by ancient thinkers like Hippocrates, but today the promoters of human expediency contest their very existence. The ultimate good cannot be established on a basis of shifting moral values which have suffered continual contradiction especially with regard to respect for human life. For the Christian the ultimate good is enshrined in the laws of God; and since the 'good action' in the context of serving those in need has received its widest and historically most consistent definition among Christians, this should be the starting point for forming a consensus on the right motivation for good action.[2]

As T. S. Eliot phrased it,

> However bigoted the announcement may sound, the Christian can be satisfied with nothing less than a Christian organization of society—which is not the same thing as a society consisting exclusively of devout Christians. It would be a society in which the natural end of man—virtue and well-being in community—is acknowledged for all, and the supernatural end—beatitude—for those who have the eyes to see it.'[3]

FUNDAMENTAL PRINCIPLES

I. The Stranger

The antecedents of the poor relief of the Early Church can be found in the social duties laid down by Jewish law: 'You shall not wrong a stranger or oppress him, for you were strangers in the land of Egypt. You shall not afflict any widow or orphan' (Ex 22:21-2). With this law and the memory of once being strangers in Egypt the Israelites were required to offer hospitality to strangers. Indeed the law is repeated for emphasis: 'You shall not oppress a stranger; you know the heart of a stranger, for you were strangers in the land of Egypt' (Ex 23:9). The two types of stranger were the wayfaring foreigner *(nokri)* and the resident alien *(ger)*, the former were considered unacceptable for assimilation whereas the latter could be gradually assimilated. A rigid exclusiveness would seem to be counter to the law and to the examples of hospitality to strangers found in Jewish tradition (Gn 18:2-8; Jg 19:16-21; 2 K

4:8-17). The hospitality afforded to the three heavenly strangers by Abraham served as a reminder that a host might find himself entertaining angels unawares.[4]

The care of the poor wayfarer is underlined: 'The stranger who sojourns with you shall be to you as a native among you, and you shall love him as yourself; for you were strangers in the land of Egypt' (Lv 19:34). This plainly condemns any hardening of attitudes towards strangers and anticipates the great commandments of Christ (compare Mk 12:31). The law demands that the gleanings from the harvest, the edges of the corn fields and the remnants of the vineyards be left for 'the poor and the wayfarer' (Lv 19:9); again this is repeated as if for emphasis (Lv 23:22).

With the advent of Christianity the Samaritan, the Gentile, the stranger and the wayfarer, together with the Jews, were all seen as the objects of God's love which made all brothers in Christ. The parable of the Good Samaritan (Lk 10: 25-37) marks this new sense of brotherhood, in which the Samaritan, the stranger and wayfarer, are to be loved as an equal, as are all men whatever their condition; moreover they are the neighbour in the great commandment (Mk 12:31).

II. Hospitality

The sacred duty of hospitality and kindness was part of Jewish tradition: 'The Lord ... loves the sojourner, giving him food and clothing. Love the sojourner therefore; for you were sojourners in the land of Egypt' (Dt 10:17–19). Judaism gave particular expression to the oriental virtue of hospitality even to the extent of entertaining strangers: 'The stranger who sojourns with you shall be to you as the native among you, and you shall love him as yourself; for you were strangers in the land of Egypt' (Lv 19:34). The reason for this hospitality is found in the book of Deuteronomy, which declares that God 'loves the sojourner, giving him food and clothing' (Dt 10:18), and Job's response is that of the righteous Jew, 'I have opened my doors to the wayfarer' (Jb 31:32).

In the Gospel our Lord is seen receiving and giving hospitality but he was criticised for eating with publicans and sinners. In such an atmosphere the 'stranger', despite the tradition of the Law, could be quite neglected. It was against this background that, when Christ deftly turned the question, Who is my neighbour?, into an instruction to go and act as a neighbour should, he told the parable of the Good Samaritan (Lk 10:25–37) in which an injured Jew is neglected by his own kind, but is shown the most exemplary hospitality by a despised Samaritan, who tends the man's wounds, and bears him to an inn, covering the expense of his stay. 'Strangers' might as attitudes hardened easily come to be regarded as enemies; to this our Lord responds, 'Love your enemies' (Mt 5:44).

Our Lord's teaching and example, in which he consorts with sinners and social outcasts such as the fallen woman (Lk 7:36-50) and Zacchaeus (Lk 19:1-10), are concerned for the perfection of hospitality. He adds that hospitality should be particularly given to those who cannot give in return, 'do good ... expecting nothing in return' (Lk 6:35), thus 'when you give a feast, invite the poor, the maimed, the lame, the blind, and you will be blessed, because they cannot repay you' (Lk 14:13-14). The apostles commended this spirit of hospitality to the followers of Christ. St Paul instructs them to 'contribute to the needs of the saints, practise hospitality' (Ro 12:13).

St Paul insists that bishops be hospitable (1 Tm 3:3; compare Ti 1:8) and he extols the perfect hospitality of Christ: 'if your enemy is hungry, feed him; if he is thirsty, give him drink' (Ro 12:20). The Letter to the Hebrews recalls Abraham's welcome of the heavenly visitors and then declares, 'Do not neglect to show hospitality to strangers, for thereby some have entertained angels unawares' (Hb 13:2). Moreover our Lord reminds us that he will say to the hospitable, 'I was a stranger ... you welcomed me' (Mt 25:35) and 'as you did it to one of these my brethren, you did it to me' (Mt 25:40).

Thus serving Christ in the 'stranger' became a new incentive for hospitality and from being a social courtesy hospitality became a witness to faith, leading St Peter to say, 'Practise hospitality ungrudgingly to one another' (1 P 4:9). The principles of Jewish social teaching are carried over into Christianity, but out of all the commandments Christ put first the commands to love God and to love one's neighbour. These two 'Great Commandments' of Jewish social teaching have shaped Christian social teaching: as Christ said 'there is no commandment greater than these' (Mk 12:31).

Notes

[1] Compare H. U. von Balthasar: 'In actively helping to alleviate the misery of their fellow human beings, in aiding their development and in attempting to storm the walls of an unjust economic order ... people experience at an existential level what it means to give oneself in faith.' See H. U. von Balthasar, *The Office of Peter and the Structure of the Church*, 2nd ed., trans. A. Emery (San Francisco, Ignatius, 1986), p. 323.

[2] 'The active habitual and detailed charity of private persons, which is so conspicuous a feature in all Christian societies, was scarcely known in antiquity ... Christianity for the first time

made charity a rudimentary virtue ... it has indissolubly united, in the minds of men, the idea of supreme goodness with that of active and constant benevolence.' See W. Lecky, *A History of European Morals from Augustus to Charlemagne*, 9th ed. (London, Longmans Green & Co., 1890), vol. 2, pp. 79–85. For a more recent assessment of charitable provision in the ancient world, see A. R. Hands, *Charities and Social Aid in Greece and Rome* (London, Thames and Hudson, 1968). Christian contributions to the debate over what was new in Christian teaching about charity include J. E. Canavan, Charity in the Early Church, in *Studies: An Irish Quarterly Review*, vol. 12, no. 45 (March 1923), pp. 61-77, and F. B. Bird, A Comparative Study of the Work of Charity in Christianity and Judaism, in *The Journal of Religious Ethics*, vol. 10, no. 1 (Spring 1982), pp. 144–169.

3   T. S. Eliot, *The Idea of a Christian Society* (London, Faber & Faber Ltd, 1939), pp. 33–34.

4   According to Jewish legend, when Abraham planted the tamarisk tree in Beersheba (Gn 21:33) he became the first person to build an inn for the reception of travellers. See S. S. Kottek, The Hospital in Jewish History, in *Reviews of Infectious Diseases*, vol. 3, no. 4 *Nosocomial Infection Control* (Jul–Aug 1981), p. 636.

CHAPTER 2

'Shelter the Homeless Poor': The Teaching of Scripture and its Application

These words (Is 58:7) underline the obligation of the pious Jew to give hospitality to the poor stranger at his gate. This respect for poor strangers is enshrined in Exodus: 'You shall not wrong a stranger or oppress him, for you are strangers in the land of Egypt. You shall not afflict any widow or orphan' (Ex 22:22–3). The memory of being strangers in Egypt was thus a reason for being sympathetic to strangers. Moreover as if for emphasis the exhortation is repeated: 'You shall not oppress a stranger: you know the heart of a stranger, for you were strangers in the land of Egypt' (Ex 23:9). Both types of stranger, the wayfaring foreigner and the resident alien, should receive hospitality as stipulated in the law: 'The stranger who sojourns with you shall be to you as a native among you, and you shall love him as yourself; for you were strangers in the land of Egypt' (Lv 19:34).

The laws of mercy extended also to those who had fallen on hard times:

> And if your brother becomes poor, and cannot maintain himself with you, you shall maintain him; as a stranger and a sojourner he shall live with you. Take no interest from him or increase, but fear your God; that your brother may live beside you. You shall not lend him your money

at interest nor give him your food for profit (Lv 25:35–7).

Hospitality was a sacred duty: 'The Lord ... loves the sojourner, giving him food and clothing. Love the sojourner therefore; for you were sojourners in Egypt' (Dt 10:17–19). It would seem that in theory Jewish social teaching had a universal application, but in practice a distinction might be made in its application to foreigners, despite the prophets' emphasizing its universal message. It was not till the coming of Christ that the Law was truly fulfilled: 'Think not that I have come to abolish the Law and the prophets; I have come not to abolish them but to fulfil them' (Mt 5:17). In the teaching of Christ love of neighbour is the necessary corollary of love of God, for it is on both that the rest of the Law depends (Mt 22:37–40).

This doctrine of hospitality is perhaps most eloquently interpreted in the parable of the Good Samaritan. 'A man was going down from Jerusalem to Jericho, and he fell among robbers, who stripped him and beat him, and departed leaving him half dead' (Lk 10:30). Our Lord in this parable goes on to describe the priest and the Levite who passed by the injured man on the other side. These official interpreters of the Law ignored their obligations, but a despised Samaritan showed mercy, caring immediately for the injured man and giving him hospitality for as long as he needed. This parable re-establishes the universal law of mercy that was enshrined in Judaism. A new sense of brotherhood dawned in Christ in which the Samaritan (the foreigner), the stranger and the wayfarer were all to be loved on equal terms as should all people whatever their condition.

The Israelite's creed began 'A wandering Aramean was my father' (Dt 26:5) and his status as God's wayfarer made him only a tenant in the land of Canaan, for he was but a 'passing guest, a sojourner' like all his fathers (Ps 39:12; compare 119:19). Abraham called himself a stranger and a sojourner (Gn 23:4) and St Paul addresses his fellow Christians in similar terms: they have no lasting home on earth (2 Co 5:1), as their true home is in heaven and only there will they cease to be strangers and thus become fellow citizens with the saints.

Christ identified with the wayfarer and stranger when he declared 'foxes have holes, and birds of the air have nests; but the Son of Man has nowhere to lay his head' (Mt 8:20). The truly righteous Jew therefore could say with Job 'I have opened my doors to strangers' (Jb 31:32), and indeed Abraham in his hospitality to strangers 'entertained angels unawares' (Heb 13:1; cf. Gn 18:1–8). It was to be expected therefore that the promised Messiah would be known for his compassion for the poor and needy, and when John the Baptist sent messengers from his prison cell to enquire whether Christ was the expected one, he received this reply: 'The blind receive their sight, the lame walk, lepers are cleansed and the deaf hear, the dead are raised up, the poor have good news preached to them' (Lk 7:22). Christ not only associated with the poor, sick, homeless, and hungry; he actually identified with them in a most dramatic way:

> For I was hungry and you gave me food, I was thirsty and you gave me drink, I was a stranger and you welcomed me, I was naked and you clothed me, I was sick and you visited me, I was in prison and you came to me' (Mt 25:35–6).

Christ will be the judge of how Christians have performed such works of mercy: 'Truly, I say to you, as you did it not to one of the least of these, you did it not unto me' (Mt 25:40).

Christianity after the example of Christ was to perfect the law rather than abolish it. Christianity continued with greater emphasis the concern for widows and orphans: 'Religion that is pure and undefiled before God the Father is this: to visit orphans and widows in their affliction' (Jm 1:27). That which was surplus to the Christian community's needs (Ac 4:32–5) was contributed to a special fund for the poor and needy, administered by specially appointed deacons (Ac 6:1–6). Again this was to perfect the teaching of the law (Dt 15:11), but the Christians sought to practise the same charity to all: 'There is neither slave nor free, there is neither male nor female; for you are all one in Christ Jesus' (Ga 3:28). St Peter declared to the infant Church, 'Practise hospitality ungrudgingly to one another,' (1 P 4:9) and his instructions were followed so well that 'there was not a needy person among them' (Ac 4:34).

The picture described in Acts was certainly in keeping with an exemplary application of Christian living, but was to some extent confined to Jerusalem; in other churches there is not found the same communal possession of property. So great were the demands of administering poor relief in the Church at Jerusalem that seven deacons were appointed, and it was the succession of deacons over the next five hundred years who had a large part in administering the Church's hospitality. Under the local bishops, who bore the ultimate responsibility, the deacons were appointed, usually seven to a bishop after the example of Jerusalem. They would administer the poor fund, keep lists of the poor of the local Church, and visit them to ascertain their needs. To facilitate this administration districts were allocated to each deacon, for example there were fourteen districts in Rome with each deacon having charge of two districts. In the early Church everything centred on the bishop who presided over the local church in each town. He would ensure that hospitality was given to the homeless and that provision was made for the needy; assisting him would be the seven deacons and an order of pious women known as 'widows' or 'deaconesses.'[1]

During the first four centuries of Christianity the Church was harried by vicious persecution at the hands of the Roman emperors and afflicted by the heresies of Marcionism, Montanism and Gnosticism. In Rome public preaching was forbidden and worship was in secret for fear of arrest, torture and death. Despite this the 'Church, in the first three centuries, succeeded not only to survive but also expand rapidly.'[2] The reason for this is plain: the persecuted and underground Church preached the silent sermon of the corporal works of mercy. The hungry were fed, the thirsty given drink, the homeless welcomed, the naked clothed, the sick and those in prison visited—and when they asked why they were treated thus the Christians told them about Christ.

This was the most effective form of evangelism as is well attested by pagan and Christian authors alike. St Justin (c. 100–c. 165), a philosopher who converted to Christianity and was later martyred, in his *Apology* writes:

> We, who loved above all else the ways of acquiring riches and possessions, now hand over to a

community fund what we possess and share it with every needy person.³

Tertullian (c. 160–c. 220), a lawyer from Carthage who converted to Christianity, wrote in his *Apology*:

> Even if we have a kind of treasury, this is not filled up from a sense of obligation, as of a hired religion. Each member adds a small sum once a month, or when he pleases, and only if he is willing and able; for no one is forced, but each contributes of his own free will. These are the deposits as it were made by devotion. For that sum is disbursed not on banquets nor drinking bouts nor unwillingly on eating-houses, but on the supporting and burying of the poor, and on boys and girls deprived of property and parents, and on aged servants of the house, also on shipwrecked persons, and any, who are in the mines or on islands or in prisons, provided it be for the cause of God's religion, who thus become pensioners of their confession. But the working of that kind of love most of all brands us with a mark of blame in the eyes of some. 'See,' they say, 'how they love one another'; for they themselves hate one another; 'and how they are ready to die for one another;' for they will be more ready to kill one another.⁴

These gifts, after being offered to God, were distributed by the deacons to the needy present. The deacons would subsequently visit those who were not present. This was all under the local bishop's direction.⁵

Poor travellers were always given hospitality. The *Didache* or *The Teaching of the Twelve Apostles*, an anonymous work dating from the late first century, contains general regulations, guidance on worship, and social teaching. The social teaching embraces the early instruction of Leviticus on hospitality and the sharing of material benefits, and it stresses the need for almsgiving and for the showing of consideration to slaves. It calls for 'everyone who comes in the Name of the Lord' to be received.[6] Similarly, in a contemporary work entitled *The Shepherd*, the author, an otherwise unknown Christian called Hermas, refers to those who 'never separated from God, but bore the Name gladly, and gladly received into their houses the servants of God.'[7]

The Christians of Rome were renowned for the help that they gave to Christians from abroad. Dionysius, bishop of Corinth c. 170, wrote as follows to the Romans,

> For from the beginning it has been your practice to do good to all the brethren in various ways, and to send contributions to many churches in every city. Thus, relieving the want of the needy, and making provision for the brethren in the mines by the gifts which you have sent from the beginning, you Romans keep up the hereditary customs of the Romans, which your blessed bishop Soter has not only maintained, but also added to, furnishing an abundance of supplies to the saints, and encouraging the brethren from abroad with blessed words, as a loving father his children.[8]

The private duty of hospitality to the poor had in this way become the major concern of the local bishop and his assistants resulting in a full programme of social welfare.

The letters of St Cyprian (d. 258), bishop of Carthage, illustrate the role of the bishop. We find him writing to his presbyters and deacons:

> I request that you will diligently take care of the widows, and of the sick, and of all the poor. Moreover, you may supply the expenses for strangers, if any should be indigent, from my own portion, which I have left with Rogatianus, our fellow presbyter.[9]

In another letter, he writes to the bishops of Numidia:

> Our brotherhood, considering all these things according to your letter, and sorrowfully examining, have all promptly and willingly and liberally gathered together supplies of money for the brethren ... We have then sent you a sum of 100,000 sesterces, which have been collected here in the Church over which by the Lord's mercy we preside, by the contributions of the clergy and people established with us, which you will there dispense with what diligence you may.[10]

Notes

[1] G. Ratzinger, *Der Geschichte Kirchlichen Armenpflege* (Freiburg, Freiburg Univ., 1884), p. 30. See also L. Lallemand, *Histoire de la Charite* (Paris, 1902–12), vol. 2, pp. 27–30.

[2] P. C. Phan, *Social Thought* (Wilmington, Delaware., M. Glazier, 1984), p. 21.

[3] St Justin, *Apologia, I, 4*, from *The First Apology, the Second Apology, the Dialogue with Trypho, Exhortations to the Greeks, Discourse to the Greeks, the Monarchy or the Rule of God, by St Justin Martyr*, trans. T. B. Falls (Washington, Catholic University of America Press, 1977). Quoted by P. C. Phan, p. 21.

[4] Tertullian, *Apology, 39*, from *Q. Septimi Florentis Tertulliani Apologeticus*, ed. F. Oehler, annotated by J. E. B. Mayor, trans. A. Souter (Cambridge, Cambridge University Press, 1917), p. 8.

[5] P. C. Phan, p. 21.

[6] *Didache*, XII, 1–2, trans. P. C. Phan, p. 45.

7 Hermas, *The Shepherd*, Sim. VIII, 10[76]:3, from *The Apostolic Fathers*, ed & trans J. B. Lightfoot and J. R. Harmer (London, MacMillan and Co, 1891), p. 459.

8 Eusebius, *Ecclesiastical History*, IV, 23.9–10, in *Eusebius: Church History, Life of Constantine the Great etc.* trans. by A. C. McGiffert and others. (Oxford, 1890), p. 88. Soter was Pope around 167–175.

9 *Letter* 35 in *The Writings of Cyprian, Bishop of Carthage*, trans. R. E. Wallis, vol. 1 (Edinburgh, T. & T. Clark, 1868), p. 100.

10 *Letter* 59:3, ibid., pp. 200–201. Writing to his presbyters and deacons, he says elsewhere, 'In respect of means, moreover, for meeting the expenses, whether for those who, having confessed their Lord with a glorious voice, have been put in prison, or for those who are labouring in poverty and want, and still stand fast in the Lord, I entreat that nothing be wanting' (*Letter* 4:1, *ibid.*, p. 18); and, 'In the meantime let the poor be taken care of as much and as well as possible; but especially those who have stood with unshaken faith and have not forsaken Christ's flock, ... And although I know that very many of those have been maintained by the vow and by the love of the brethren, yet if there be any who are in want either of clothing or maintenance, let them be supplied, with whatever things are necessary' (*Letter* 5:2, *ibid.*, pp. 20–21).

CHAPTER 3

GOSPEL ETHIC

THE THREE FOUNDATIONS of Jewish teaching, the law, worship, and the practice of mercy, find their echo in the Sermon on the Mount. Christ prefaces his sermon:

> Do not imagine that I have come to abolish the law or the prophets. I have come not to abolish but to complete them. I tell you solemnly, till heaven and earth disappear, not one dot, not one little stroke, shall disappear from the law until its purpose is achieved (Mt 5:17–18).

The old law is thus enshrined in the new. Christ outlines the new law (Mt 5:17–48) and the new approach to worship (Mt 6:1–34), and expands the teaching on the practice of mercy as follows:

> Do not judge, and you will not be judged, because the judgements you give are the judgements you will get, and the amount you measure out is the amount you will be given. Why do you observe the splinter in your brother's eye and never notice the plank in your own? How dare you say to your brother, 'Let me take the splinter out of your eye', when all the time there is a plank in your own? Hypocrite! Take the plank out of your own eye first, and then you will see clearly enough to take the splinter out of your brother's eye.
>
> Do not give dogs what is holy; and do not throw your pearls in front of pigs, or they may trample

> them and turn on you and tear you to pieces. Ask and it will be given you; search, and you will find; knock, and the door will be opened to you. For the one who asks always receives; the one who searches always finds; the one who knocks will always have the door opened to him. Is there a man among you who would hand his son a stone when he asked for bread? Or would hand him a snake when he asked for a fish? If you, then, who are evil, know how to give your children what is good, how much more will your Father in heaven give good things to those who ask him!
>
> So always treat others as you would like them to treat you; that is the meaning of the Law and the prophets (Mt 7:1–12).

This new teaching underlines the need for right relations as a practical expression of the commandment to love one's neighbour as oneself. It thus enhances the old teaching, providing an even greater sense of communal solidarity and mutual support. The caveat against self-righteousness comes first, guarding against condescension, ensuring purity of motive (what the Mishnah terms *kavanah*), and proscribing hypocrisy. The first consideration in practising mercy and loving-kindness towards one's neighbour is to be without condescension and a patronising approach. Indiscriminate action, however, can destroy its own ends, and reckless giving can create dependence and devalue the quality of consideration, like giving holy things to dogs. There is in other words an authentic kindness that respects the recipient's self determination and avoids the excess that blunts the edge of discerning concern. Finally, echoing the commandment to love one's neighbour as oneself, we should treat others as we wish to be treated ourselves.

The teachings of the Sermon on the Mount are contained in essence in the Beatitudes (Mt 5:3–12). These are not strictly blessings but states of blessedness equated with the Kingdom of Heaven; these states of blessedness are granted to the poor in spirit, the gentle, those who mourn, those who hunger and thirst for what is right, the merciful, the pure in heart, the peacemakers and those persecuted in the cause of right. Rabbi Gerald Friedlander commented,

> The Beatitudes have undoubtedly a lofty tone, but let us not forget that all that they teach can be found in Isaiah and the Psalms. Israel finds nothing new here. The Jew rejoices to think that such fine teaching is common to Judaism and Christianity.[1]

In the first Beatitude the Greek word used to mean 'poor in spirit' is *ptochos*, a word which means destitute, and is the word used to describe the beggar Lazarus (Lk 16:20–21) and the wayfarers brought in from the highways as unforeseen guests at the great banquet in Luke (Lk 14:21). St James uses *ptochos* to describe the poor man in the synagogue who, in an example of flawed judgement, is ignored in favour of one splendidly dressed (Jm 2:2–3).

For the pagan world, it was a shameful thing to be *ptochos*; the *ptochos* disfigured the state or city where he was to be found; and the word *ptochos* was invariably used in a derogatory sense. However Christ drew on the tradition of the Jewish scriptures, where the Hebrew word for poor was *'ani* (plural *'aniyyim*), a word which initially meant simply a poor man, but came to imply one who is also defenceless and on the margins of society, and then to mean the poor ones who were faithful to God and looked forward to divine deliverance; thus in the Psalms God is described as the *poor man's* deliverer (Psalms 34:6; 35:10; 40:17; 72:2). Christ, coming not to abolish but to complete the law, referred to the lowly poor ones favoured by God, who look for divine redemption and to whom the Kingdom of Heaven belongs (Mt 5:3).[2]

In the second Beatitude those who sorrow or mourn will be comforted (Mt 5:4), and their sorrow, like the sorrow of Lazarus the beggar, will be turned to joy (Lk 16:25). It is the joy of the future, the treasure laid up in heaven, which the *'aniyyim* await in their present sorrow; a sorrow compared to that of Christ. 'Can there be any sorrow like my sorrow?' (Lm 1:12).[3]

In the third Beatitude the gentle or meek will have 'the earth for their heritage' rather than material reward (Mt 5:4). The Hebrew word corresponding to meek is *'anaw* (plural *'anawim*), and may be related to *'ani*. This again is derived from the teaching of the Old Testament: 'the humble will have the land for their own' (Ps 37:11). Such people rely on God's persistence and are without resentment at their lot in life, for whatever happens, with faith all things can work together for good. God listens to the gentle or humble and guides them in the right way (Ps 9:12; 10:17; 25:9; 69:32). The corresponding Greek word is *präus* which suggests not so much easy-going tolerance as control and resilience, a gentleness that has its source in strength and submission to God's will. Mary's 'Behold the handmaid of the Lord: be it unto me according to your word' (Lk 1:38), sums up the attitude of the *anawim*. Christ's invitation to take up one's cross and follow him is part of this acceptance which involves a share in his sorrow.[4]

In the fourth Beatitude those who hunger and thirst for righteousness (in Greek, *dikaiosune*) and will be satisfied (Mt 5:6) are those who strive for justice, but also for right-living and for justification by faith. Right-living indicates an obligation to take action and equates with the striving induced by hunger and thirst. Justice can be interpreted as God's will with the contemporary application of social justice, which in the letter of St James produces those works which indicate the justification by faith.[5] Those who are unable to rest content with unequal social conditions, and who out of love for God seek to remedy the lot of the poor who 'will be satisfied'—this is social justice. Justification in this context is to accept a person as he is (cf. the Prodigal Son), to restore the relationship between God and man. As God in His mercy accepts us the way we are, so ought we to accept one another.[6]

In the fifth Beatitude the merciful will 'have mercy shown them' (Mt 5:7) and mercy (in Hebrew, *chesed*) is really the key to social teaching in the Bible. Rather than meaning mitigation of sentence, biblical mercy refers to loving kindness and in particular the action of God, and his relationship with man. God's mercy is everlasting (Ps 89:1–2; 100:5; 103:17; 106:1; 107:1; 136:1–26; 138:8). God's action in history (salvation history), such as the exodus from Egypt, is seen as his mercy (his favour). Mercy is the basis of man's relationship with God; in justice fallen man deserves to die but in God's mercy he is raised up and he is told to ask for mercy (not justice), the basis of man's appeal for forgiveness (Ps 6:4; 31:16).[7] Rabbi Simeon ben Gamaliel saw *chesed* as a personal and spontaneous outgoing love, vital to the continuance of the world: 'On three things the world is stayed; on the Thorah, and on the Worship, and on the bestowal of Kindnesses.'[8]

Chesed in its original application meant 'truth' as well as mercy and loving-kindness: this is a Biblical idiom in which truth means faithfulness; as the psalmist says, 'Mercy and Truth have met' (Ps 85:10). This bespeaks God's covenant relationship of enduring love with his people. Mercy is invariably linked with justice (Ho 12:6; Mi 6:8; Zc 7:9). The Greek word for mercy is *eleos*[9] which recalls the word *elaion*, the word for the oil or balm with which a wound might be soothed, and *eleos* occurs linked with justice (Mt 23:22; Jm 2:13). Thus in the parable of the Good Samaritan (Lk 10:29–37) the Samaritan pours oil into the wounds of the injured man to soothe the hurt. To our Lord's question, Who was neighbour to the man who fell among thieves the reply was bound to be 'the one who showed mercy' (Lk 10:37). The Gospel ethic is inseparable from justice with mercy, the foundations of social doctrine in the new dispensation. As Christ told the Pharisees, who being obsessed with the letter of the law had neglected the weightier matters of justice and mercy (Mt 23:23) — this implies their neglect of the poor. Our Lord had come to 'complete' the law; for 'not one dot, not one little stroke, shall disappear from the law until its purpose is achieved' (Mt 5:18).

Thus it was that Christians taught 'mercy', the word that becomes *caritas* in Latin and social justice in our own day, for a world without mercy is a world without Christ. In our own day cruelty still shocks those brought up in the Christian faith and the Church, far from having taught the world mercy, still has much to do in changing mankind by example. This mercy is unselfish and identifies with the sufferer, as seen in Christ, who became one with us and who out of mercy saved us by his cross. The justice of God is mercy, as Paul implies (Ro 3:21–6; 10:3), and mankind will be judged on the practice of mercy (Mt 6:14–15; 7:2; Jm 2:13); God has shown us his mercy, and we are told that we will be judged on how we have shown mercy to the poor and needy (Mt 25:34–46). Mercy therefore implies an identification or solidarity with the poor and needy, a solidarity with the underprivileged, whose practical results are care and support for the sufferer, something which anticipates the distributive or social justice of modern times.

The sixth beatitude, 'Blessed are the pure in heart for they shall see God' (Mt 5:8), surely indicates the beatific vision. However Christ taught that 'if your eye is single your body will be full of light' (Mt 6:22) which suggests a single-minded concern for the poor so as to see Christ in them, which he implies as the way to salvation (Mt 25:31–46). The pure in heart (in Greek, *katharoi*) shall see God, and purity is used mostly in the Bible to mean ritual purity. Ritual purity is what the Pharisees had, but as Our Lord said they were 'whited sepulchres,' concealing dead men's bones (Mt 23:27–8). The purity of the beatitude means more than this; the psalmist speaks of a purity of heart (Ps 24:4) but he means something more than chastity: he means a single-mindedness, a unity of purpose. In caring for the poor there could be the element of self-advertisement to court public esteem. This purity applies therefore also to motive.[10]

In the seventh Beatitude, the peacemakers will be called 'sons of God' (Mt 5:9); here peace is much more than the cessation of war. Peace (in Hebrew, *shalom*) indicates social content and right relationship, something which always needs a striving to achieve. The Greek word is *eirene* and is frequently used throughout as a greeting—a state which Christ wills and as a foretaste to the future Kingdom—hence his greeting before ascending to his Father, 'Peace I bequeath to you, my own peace I give you' (Jn 14:27). Thus there are many situations which call out for redress in the world and in the Church. In the Church this is a scandal because a bogus peace can exist in supporting the *status quo*. The reform of the episcopal and priestly ministry is a thorny topic and rarely addressed, and yet for social doctrine to be made known there must be reform in order to reveal the practical side of evangelism. Herein lies the work of the peacemakers, seeking to change inherited traditions which are an obstacle to right relationships. Renewal in the Church perforce requires a restoration of first principles, principles by which the early Christians, under their bishops, taught the world about poor relief. *Shalom*, also means welfare: peacemakers are therefore those who seek the 'common good,' the work of social reform. To seek everyone's welfare is to identify all as 'Sons of God.'[11]

This Beatitude was understood by St Clement of Alexandria (c. 150–c. 215) to refer to 'those who have stilled the incredible battle which goes on in their own souls,' whereas St Augustine (354–430), bishop of Hippo, understood it to be a blessing on those 'who have composed and subjected to reason all the motions of their minds, and who have tamed their carnal desires.'[12] This is the peace which St Paul saw as resolving the war in his members (Rm 7:21–5), the peace of Christ which the world cannot give. There is also the peace of right relationships within society across boundaries of class, race and religion—in this the Good Samaritan is a peacemaker. The right relationship with God enables right relationships within society.

In the eighth Beatitude, the Kingdom of Heaven is promised to those who are persecuted in the cause of right. Christianity demanded a distinct way of life that stood out against the pagan world. Christ told his followers to take up their cross (Mt 16:24) and follow him; to share their Master's suffering. Inevitably, refusing to offer incense to the Emperor and eschewing pagan custom set Christians apart and made them objects of ridicule and persecution. As St Paul would say, 'if to live is Christ then to die is' to gain the Kingdom of Heaven (Ph 1:21).

Forbidden to preach or to worship in public the early Church preached by example, caring for the needy, acting on spontaneous love to seek right relations and to show solidarity with all who suffered. The Gospel ethic looked back to Judaism and forward to future comfort, but meanwhile Christians strove to manifest God's will in works of mercy, single-minded in their dedication to reconcile all men despite the cost. God's loving kindness or mercy had been shown them, and so in the words of the New Commandment they sought to love one another as God in Christ had loved them.

> Be merciful as your Father is merciful. Do not judge, and you will not be judged; do not condemn, and you will not be condemned; pardon and you will be pardoned. Give, and

you will be given a full measure, pressed down, shaken together and running over (Lk 6:36–38).

The *Didache* has this to say about almsgiving:-

> Give to everybody who begs from you, without looking for any repayment, for the Father wants that we should share his gracious bounty to all men. A giver who gives freely, as the commandment bid him, is blessed, for he is guiltless. But woe to the receiver! If he receives because he is in need, he is guiltless. But if he is not in need, he will be required to show why he received and for what purpose. He will be thrown into prison and his action will be investigated, and he will not get out until he has paid the last penny.[13]

Such strictures are surprising and the mediaeval poor law makes no such conditions. The *Didache* refers later to hospitality:

> If the newcomer is only passing through, assist him as much as you can. But he must not stay with you more than two days, or, if necessary, three. If he wants to settle down among you, and if he is a skilled worker, he must work for his living. If, however, he knows no trade, use your judgement to make sure that he does not live in idleness on the pretext he is a Christian. If he refuses to do this, he is only trying to exploit Christ. You must be on your guard against such people.[14]

Pope St Clement I, bishop of Rome c. 96, writing to the Corinthians, has this to say about solidarity:

> In Christ Jesus, then, we must preserve this corporate body of ours in its entirety. Each must

be subject to his neighbour, according to his special gifts. The strong are not to ignore the weak, and the weak should respect the strong. The rich must provide for the poor, and the poor should thank God for giving him someone to meet his needs.[15]

This idea of solidarity is found in the Talmud as well as in Acts (compare the Beatitudes) and the relationship between benefactor and recipient was spelt out by Pope St Gregory I (c. 540–604) in his *Sermon on the Rich Man and Lazarus:*

> The poor come unsought to crowd upon us and beg; and these are those who will one day be our intercessors. It is we who should do the asking, and yet they ask of us. Ought we to refuse the request when those who make it are our advocates?[16]

The prayer with which St Clement concludes his letter to the Corinthians shows the depth of the apostolic Church's concern for the poor:

> We beseech you, O Lord, be our Helper and Protector. Rescue the afflicted, pity the lowly, raise up the fallen, assist the needy, heal the sick, bring back those of your people who stray, feed the hungry, release our captives, support the weak, comfort the faint-hearted. Let all the nations realize that you are the only God, that Jesus Christ is your Child, and that we are your people and the sheep of your pasture.[17]

Bishop Dionysius of Corinth described how in second century Rome the Christians welcomed the poor and the homeless[18] and it was during the first three hundred years of persecution that Christianity saw its most rapid expansion. Solidarity remains a specialized term in the Church's social doctrine today.

Notes

1. G. Friedlander, *The Jewish Sources of the Sermon on the Mount* (London, George Routledge & Sons Ltd, 1911), p. 23.
2. See W. Barclay, *The Plain Man Looks at the Beatitudes* (London, Fontana, 1965), pp. 16–24, with his discussion of the meaning of *ptochos*, pp. 18–19, and M. Mollat, *The Poor in the Middle Ages: An Essay in Social History*, trans. from the French by A. Goldhammer (New Haven and London, Yale University Press, 1986), p. 17.
3. See W. Barclay, pp. 25–33.
4. See W. Barclay, pp. 34–43, and his discussion of the meaning of *praus*, pp. 34–39.
5. Paul uses *dikaiosune* as justification by faith (Rm 4:25).
6. See W. Barclay, pp. 44–55.
7. For the meaning of *chesed*, see W. Barclay, pp. 56–71.
8. *Pirqe Aboth* 1.2, in *Sayings of the Jewish Fathers, Comprising Pirqe Aboth and Pereq R. Meir, ...* by C. Taylor (Cambridge, Cambridge University Press, 1877). For a study of the later development of Jewish charitable teaching and practice, see M. R. Cohen, *Poverty and Charity in the Jewish Community of Medieval Egypt* (Princeton and Oxford, Princeton University Press, 2005).
9. The corresponding verb is found in *Kyrie eleison* (Lord have mercy).
10. See W. Barclay, pp. 72–81.
11. For the meaning of *shalom*, see W. Barclay, pp. 82–96.
12. Quoted *ibid.* p. 85.
13. *Didache*, I, 5. trans. P. C. Phan, p. 45.
14. *Didache*, XII, 2–5, trans. P. C. Phan, p. 46.
15. *1 Clement* XXXVIII, 1–22, trans. P. C. Phan, p. 47.
16. Homily XL, 10, on Lk 16:19–31, trans. P. C. Phan, p. 266.
17. *1 Clement* LIX, 4, trans. P. C. Phan, p. 47.
18. See above, p. 15.

CHAPTER 4

THE POOR AND THE WRITINGS OF THE FATHERS

THE FATHERS OF the Church possessed a social doctrine but not one that they had produced by their own philosophising, for Christianity in its essence possesses a unique social consciousness.[1] This social doctrine was devised in the light of the teaching of Christ and his Apostles, mediated through Christian tradition and scripture. The Jewish Law of the Old Testament was a much greater influence than were ancient philosophies such as Platonism and Stoicism.

The Church's beginnings after Pentecost give a vivid picture of a shared Gospel life, in which everything is held in common, any other possessions being sold so as to distribute more equitably to those in need (Ac 2:44–45). The care of the poor and weak was paramount. Moreover the first members of the church not only worshipped together, they also fed together, each Christian household taking turns to be host: and they 'took their share of food with gladness and simplicity of heart, praising God, and winning favour with all the people. And each day the Lord added to their fellowship others that were to be saved' (Ac 2:46–47, Knox translation).

This description of early Christian life records the infant Church's existence in the city of Jerusalem, a small area compared with some of the sprawling parishes of our own day and yet still an inspiring model; each congregation had a fund for the relief of the poor and would give to other congregations in need (Ac 11:29). However the early Christian groupings, although bearing the names of Galatia, Corinth or Rome, were hardly to be compared in size to modern dioceses. Each local Church would have in time its own elder called a bishop, for which the Greek word (*episkopos*, meaning someone who had oversight) was derived from the overseer of the poor (*episkopos ton ptochon*) attached to a synagogue. This situation of the community sharing a common life centred on the bishop was typical of all the early dioceses, thus reproducing to some extent the form of life which Our Lord shared with his twelve Apostles.[2] The bishop presiding over his respective community supervised its worship, discipline and rule of life, creating a society held together by purely spiritual bonds.

However, the Church at Alexandria, traditionally founded by St Mark the Evangelist, developed a superior position over the local Churches of Egypt such as Thinuis and Pentapolis of Cyrene, so that the Bishop of Alexandria had jurisdiction over the other local bishops.[3] In time this hierarchic principle, which developed and built up the church, would give rise to the distinctions of bishop and archbishop, but at this early stage the principal bishop's role was most akin to that of patriarch, having a measure of autonomy which the distance between other Church groupings necessitated. As the Church's organic unity developed and local Christian communities became more integrated parts of the whole, this independence lessened.

Bishops by their consecration oath were especially bound to 'show mercy and kindness, for the name of the Lord to the poor, the stranger and all in want,' and in the post-apostolic period there is ample evidence that this was taken seriously. Gifts for the poor were brought to the altar at the offertory in the Sunday Mass, to be dispensed later by the bishop; St Clement encouraged and commended the Corinthian Christians for their hospitality;[4] and the Christian philosopher Aristides (2nd century) wrote, 'when [the Christians] see a stranger, they take him in to their homes and rejoice over him as a very brother; for they do not call them brethren after the flesh, but brethren after the spirit and in God.'[5]

St Cyprian well represents the social concern of the early bishops. He was so concerned for poor wayfarers that he instructed his presbyters and deacons to take over their care during his absence.[6] In one work he imagines the Devil challenging Christ to a contest, saying to him, 'There among your poor you are clothed and you are fed, you promise those who give alms eternal life ...'[7] St John Chrysostom (c. 347–407), bishop of Constantinople, boasted that the community of Antioch cared for three thousand widows, wayfarers and sick daily, and he inveighed against riches in his exposition of Mt 6:16;[8] while the concern of bishops generally for the poor was such that by the fourth century hospices, or houses of hospitality, were being established in the dioceses for wayfarers, pilgrims, foundlings, orphans, the aged and the sick.

Hospitality was considered an important duty of the bishop: as the *Didascalia Apostolorum*, a summary of church practice composed probably in the third century, put it:

> And let his hand be open to give; and let him love the orphans with the widows, and be a lover of the poor and of strangers. And let him

be alert in his ministry, and constant in ministration; and let him be afflicting his soul, and not be one that is put to confusion. And let him know who is the more worthy to receive; for if there be a widow who has somewhat, or is able to nourish herself with that which she needs for her bodily sustenance; and there be another who, though she is not a widow, is in want, whether by reason of sickness, or of the rearing of children, or of bodily infirmity: to this latter rather let him stretch out his hand. But if there be any man who is dissolute, or drunken, or idle, and he be in straits for bodily nourishment, the same is not worthy of an alms, neither of the Church.[9]

St Basil the Great (c. 330–379) wrote, 'The bread in your hoard belongs to the hungry, the cloak in your wardrobe belongs to the naked, the shoes you let rot belong to the barefoot, the money in your vaults belongs to the destitute.'[10]

Although hospitality was the special duty of the bishops, deacons were often assigned to act in their stead. Deacons, who in the Acts of the Apostles were first selected to look after the common purse and care for widows, thus in addition to their liturgical functions came to care for the homeless and to administer the Church's poor relief. As the *Didascalia Apostolorum* taught, 'let the deacons go in to those who are in distress, and let them visit each one and provide him with what he lacks.'[11] The early Christians used the Latin word *caritas* to describe these works, with the result that the modern understanding of charity or charitable work, is derived from the traditional term for mercy and loving kindness.

St Gregory of Nyssa (c. 330–395), in his *Fifth Sermon on the Beatitudes*, applies the traditional understanding of mercy to social need, making a practical application of the Beatitudes:

> Now what is mercy, and in regard to what is it practised? And how is he blessed to whom is returned what he gives? For he says: 'Blessed are the merciful, for they shall obtain mercy.' The obvious meaning of these words invites men to mutual charity and compassion, which are demanded by the capricious inequality of the circumstances of life. For not all give in the same conditions, neither as regards reputation, nor physical constitution, nor assets. Life in many ways is often divided into opposites, since it may be spent as a slave or a master, in riches or in poverty, in fame or dishonour, in bodily infirmity or in good health. Therefore the creature in need should be made equal to the one who has a larger share, and that which is lacking should be filled by what has abundance. This is the law mercy gives men in regard to the needy ... mercy is a voluntary sorrow that joins itself to the suffering of others ... mercy is a loving disposition towards those who suffer distress. For as unkindness and cruelty have their origin in hate, so mercy springs from love, without which it could not exist ... mercy is intensified charity—hence a man of such disposition of soul is truly blessed since he has reached the summit of virtue.

If there was any doubt as to how the early Christians understood the term *chesed* or mercy, here is ample evidence of its application together with an interpretation of the Beatitudes as a specific example of social doctrine. St Gregory moreover shows an understanding of Jewish social doctrine in his grasp of the spiritual disposition necessary for a good action, that is the necessary disposition of mind and heart, the necessary intention focused, without selfish motives, on God's will. St Gregory upholds the right intention and disposition as virtuous, even if the action is prevented. This also bespeaks a right relationship with God and man so that the action is performed for its own sake. St Gregory continues,

> Let no one think that this virtue is concerned solely with material things; else it could be attained only by someone who has the necessary means for doing good. No; it seems to me more adequate to place such virtue in the choice of will. For if a man only wills the good, but is prevented from accomplishing it by lack of means, he is not inferior, as regards his state of soul, to the person who shows his intentions by works. Therefore we need not explain in detail how much we gain for our life if we understand the meaning of the Beatitude in this way. Even to those who are uneducated the advantages this counsel brings to our life should be quite obvious. If, indeed, such attitude of mind to our inferiors were innate in all of us, there would no longer be either superfluity or want. Life would no longer be lived in diametrically opposite ways; man would no longer be distressed by want or humiliated by slavery, nor would dishonour sadden him. For all things would be common to all, and man's life as a citizen would be marked by complete equality before the law since the person who was responsible for the government would of his own free will be on a level with the rest.

St Gregory goes on to describe the work of mercy taught by the rabbinical schools, as found in Leviticus and Deutoronomy, as outlined in the Gospels and the *Didache*, and as continued among the apostles, as the 'pledge of charity' *(caritas)*:

> If such a state of affairs existed, no cause would be left for enmity. Envy would be futile, hate would disappear, remembrance of injuries would be banished along with lies, fraud, and war, all of which are bred by covetousness ... and with the departure of evils there would enter instead the whole array of good things, peace and justice with all their train of virtues ... Therefore mercy is the parent of kindness, the pledge of charity, the bond of all loving disposition.[12]

Converts to Christianity, and the wealthy in particular, would frequently give all their goods to the poor. Indeed this interpretation of the simplicity of the 'Gospel life' appears to have been adopted by most believers—a dramatic contrast to modern Christians. The duty of distributing such goods was that of the bishop whose title 'father of the poor and protector of widows and orphans' was acknowledged by Church and State alike. The bishops moreover led the Church in preaching on the fundamental truths of Christian charity, and protested against excessive taxes and the harsh methods employed in collecting them, and against land-owners' oppression of tenants, the extortion of usury, the forcible enslavement of free men, the tyranny of civil officials, the injustice of the courts, and the ill-treatment of slaves, favouring their emancipation instead.

St Clement and St Cyprian moreover denounced the luxury of the times as wholly unworthy of Christians who should love their poor neighbours.[13] The Fathers of the early Church incessantly proclaimed the duties of almsgiving and of stewardship of wealth. Those who refused to distribute their superfluous goods to the needy were called 'robbers' and 'thieves' and those who practised extortion and usury were expected to make restitution. The Fathers constantly proclaimed the duty of almsgiving: almsgiving was a gift to God from the rich and a gift from God to the poor: 'Rich men should provide for the poor and the poor should thank God for giving somebody to supply their wants.'[14] The rich were told that through this practice they were merely making a return to God while the poor, seeing it as a gift from God, were enabled to accept without injury to self-respect and in a spirit of gratitude to God and to the human donor as his instrument. The poor by praying for the human donor made an equitable return and thus they too dispensed charity. The faithful gave so freely and spontaneously that exact definitions of the duty of almsgiving were not deemed necessary and funds were also received in restitution from public sinners, extortioners, unjust possessors, persons engaged in sinful occupations, and even from unbelievers.

This remarkable poor relief of the early Church was in part conditioned by the secular environment. The Christian community rejected the authority of the Roman state in matters of morality and religion and incurred the displeasure of the civil authority. They refused to offer sacrifices or to swear in the name of pagan deities and their lives became separated from the rest of society and thus excited suspicion and resentment. Persecution followed and the Christian community under such restraints came to embrace a life of prayer, fasting, chastity and martyrdom. Under such conditions donors' lack of worldly expectation made them all the readier to give alms.

The local bishops directed the administration of *caritas*, organising diligent enquiries as to people's needs, which were registered and then relieved as the bishop considered appropriate. Deacons saw to the distribution and deaconesses (unmarried women or widows) saw to the needs of women. This primitive administration of poor relief in the early Church has yet to be improved upon: as the Lutheran scholar Uhlhorn has written, 'Never has [the Church] more highly reverenced the poor, more kindly and lovingly treated them; never also has she been farther from fostering beggary, and making their life easy to idlers.'[15]

Assistance was thus afforded to clergy, widows, orphans, the destitute, the aged, the sick, the persecuted, the imprisoned, and the stranger, and a decent burial was given to the neglected dead. Never since have Our Lord's words (Mt 25:31–46) been so conscientiously implemented. After the victory of Constantine in 312 the Church obtained freedom and social importance and so was called upon to relieve the suffering of the whole population, an understanding of charity hitherto unknown in ancient Rome. In order to fund this work the Church retained the custom of oblations at Mass and collections on fast days, and added new extraordinary collections.

Constantine, once in power, was swift to enact a series of legislative provisions for the poor, one of the earliest setting up the free distribution of bread to citizens. However the generosity of the age of persecution was never to be repeated: the ministration of poor relief was now superintended by civil officers of the State. This duty was soon transferred to the administration of the Church which thereby acquired great wealth; the law of tithes was imposed to support the Church's charitable works towards the end of the sixth century; and additional revenue came from the emperors and generals of the new Christian Empire.

As in the days of persecution the relief of the poor was regarded as one of the primary functions of the Church, and indeed 'the very ample endowment of the clergy seems, to a great extent, to have been bestowed for the purpose of enabling them to perform this primary and paramount duty.'[16] Pope St Gregory I spoke of the possessions of the Church as the patrimony of the poor,[17] and recorded that a quarter of the Church's income was devoted to the poor while the remaining three quarters were retained for the local bishop, the clergy and the maintenance of church possessions.[18] The administration of the Church's poor fund remained with the bishop assisted by the *oeconomus*, usually a priest, who in turn was assisted by deacons. In every diocese there were houses called *diaconice* from which assistance was given to the poor, the sick and the aged. Moreover each diocese came to have a *xenodochion*, or *hospitium*, a place of hospitality and a forerunner of the modern hospital.

These originated in the fourth century and were primarily for the reception of wayfarers, but also took on the care of the sick, the homeless poor, widows, abandoned children and all in need. By time of Pope St Gregory I in the sixth century most cities in the Roman Empire possessed such an institution under the control of the local bishop. These 'hospitals' were supported by landed endowments, the revenues of the church and special contributions of the faithful. Private individuals, some of whose names (such as Fabiola, Pammachius, Demetrius, Zodicum, Pulcheria and Olympia) are still on record, gave large donations of property for the endowment of hospitals.

There had been a decline from the fervour of the previous age but the generosity of the faithful continued. Bishops and clergy with the wider responsibility of the Church's mission continued to emphasise the meritorious character of almsgiving and succour to the poor, thus preaching the Gospel in the Church's concern for the weak and needy.

Notes

[1] P. C. Phan, *Social Thought* (Wilmington, Delaware, M. Glazier Inc., 1984), p. 16.

[2] Thus in Eusebius' account of the martyrdom of the Christians of Lyons in 178 a prominent place is assigned to the death of their aged bishop Pothinus: Eusebius, *Ecclesiastical History*, V, 1.29–31. The word 'Church' was only given to the Mother or Cathedral Church in each case.

[3] This jurisdiction was ratified by the Council of Nicea in 325.

[4] *1 Clement* I, 2.

[5] Aristides, *Apology*, XV, from *The Apology of Aristides the Philosopher*, trans from the Greek and Syriac by D. M. Kay, The Ante-Nicene Fathers, vol. 9 (New York, Charles Scribner's Sons, 1900).

[6] See above, p. 15.

[7] St Cyprian, *Work and Alms* 22, in *St Cyprian: Treatises*, trans. and ed. by R. J. Deferrari, A. E. Keenan, M. H. Mahoney, G. E. Conway (New York, Catholic University of America, 1958), p. 248.

[8] *St John Chrysostom, Homily 20.*

[9] *Didascalia Apostolorum* IV, 2.4, in *Didascalia Apostolorum, the Syriac Version trans. and accompanied by the Verona Latin*

Fragments with an intro. and notes by R. H. Connolly (Oxford, The Clarendon Press, 1929).

10 St Basil, *Homily on Lk 12:18*, ch. 7, trans. P. C. Phan, p. 117.

11 *Didascalia Apostolorum* XVIII, 4.9.

12 St Gregory of Nyssa, *Sermon 5 on the Beatitudes*, trans. P. C. Phan, pp. 128–130.

13 G. Ratzinger, *Der Geschichte Kirchlichen Armenpflege* (Freiburg, Freiburg Univ., 1884), p. 85 f. Compare J. G. W. Uhlhorn, *Christian Charity in the Ancient Church* (New York, C. Scribner's Sons, 1881), pp. 129f.

14 *1 Clement*, XXXVIII, 2, trans. P. C. Phan, p. 47.

15 J. G. W. Uhlhorn, p. 180.

16 R. Pashley, *Pauperism and Poor Laws* (London, Longman Brown Green and Longmans, 1852), p. 135.

17 St Gregory refers to the property of the Church as 'res pauperum' or the inheritance of the poor (*Letters*, VI, 55).

18 *Letters*, XI, 64. See also J. G. W. Uhlhorn, p. 266.

CHAPTER 5

MONASTIC HOSPITALITY

CHRISTENDOM OWES THE monastic ideal to St Anthony of Egypt (c. 251–356), who took as his calling an individual response to the words of the Gospel: 'If you would be perfect, go sell all that you have and give to the poor, and come follow me and you will have treasure in heaven' (Mt 19:21). His monasticism was individual, suggesting that in his view the organized Church had become an impossible dwelling-place for anyone who wished to lead a truly Christian life. Solitary prayer, fasting and scripture study took precedence over the common life of public worship and ecclesiastical control, although Anthony remained entirely loyal to his local bishop, St Athanasius (c. 296–373). St Anthony's example was followed by St Macarius (c. 300–c. 390) and St Pachomius (c. 290–346).

St Pachomius was the first to gather individual monks together into communities, establishing nine monasteries for men, including one at Tabernis on the banks of the Nile, and two monasteries for women. Each of these communities had a guest house for the wayfarer at its portal, thus inaugurating a new and substantial contribution to the Church's hospitality. John Cassian (c. 360–435), an abbot of one such community, described the importance paid to hospitality:

> We came from Palestine into Egypt, to one of the Fathers. And he showed us hospitality, and we said to him, 'Wherefore, in welcoming the brethren dost thou not keep the rule of fasting,

as they do in Palestine?' And he made answer, 'Fasting is ever with me, but I cannot keep you ever here: and though fasting be indeed useful and necessary, it is a matter of our own choosing: but love in its fullness the law of God requires at our hands. So, receiving Christ in you, I must show you whatever things be of love, with all carefulness: but when I have sent you away, then may I take up again the rule of fasting. The children of the bridegroom do not fast while the bridegroom is with them, but when he is taken from them, then shall they fast; it is in their own power.

A brother came to a certain solitary: and when he was going away from him, he said, 'Forgive me, Father, for I have made thee break thy rule.' He made answer and said, 'My rule is to receive thee with hospitality and send thee away in peace.'[1]

Hospitality in the broad sense was part of normal human intercourse and has always been associated with the monastic tradition, this is therefore only mentioned in passing. Apostolic hospitality is understood to mean,

When you give a dinner or a banquet, do not invite your friends, or your brothers or your kinsmen or rich neighbours, lest they invite you in return and you be repaid. But when you give a feast, invite the poor, the maimed, the lame, the blind and you will be blessed, because they cannot repay you (Lk 14:12–14).

At this early stage in the Church's development 'the common life', taken on from apostolic times, gave a natural impetus to the formation of religious communities. There was little canonical distinction between the secular and religious life: indeed by the fifth century St Augustine had drawn up a rule for both men and women and favoured living the 'common life' with his clergy. His biographer Possidius wrote, 'At the same house and table together with him the clergy were regularly fed and clothed at the common expense.'[2] He gathered around him 'servants of God' in black robes, insisting that his priests lived with him. His house thus became a monastic establishment, separated from the life of the town by a strict rule including vows of poverty and chastity, obligatory vegetarianism, and a ban on female visitors. This community lived an ordered life of prayer and Bible study, many of its members becoming bishops in their turn and establishing similar communities. Augustine himself would give lavishly to the poor and on the anniversary of his ordination would throw a banquet for them. His open handed courtesy was understood as 'laying up ... a good foundation for the future' (1 Tm 6:19) and the hospitality of his table would not permit an uncharitable word. He thus gave renewed emphasis to the original understanding that a bishop was an *episcopos* or overseer of charity. His community was however a living criticism of ecclesiastical society and of certain bishops who bore their office like a temporal honour.

This experience of the Christian 'common life' was the basis of the Rules of St Basil and St Augustine; when St Benedict (c. 480–c. 550) came to form his monastic Rule, he drew on this early tradition and in particular on Cassian's *Institutes*, which set out the ordinary rules of monastic life. Like St Anthony and St Pachomius before him, St Benedict started his vocation as a solitary (at Subiaco in Northern Italy) and others, attracted by his life, came to join him. His Rule, as earlier monastic traditions did, shows special concern for hospitality. It quotes the text, 'I was a stranger and you took me in' (Mt 25:35) and reminds the monks that Christ will repeat these words on the last day to each one of them:

> All guests who present themselves are to be welcomed as Christ, for He Himself will say: 'I was a stranger and you welcomed me' [Mt 25:35]. Proper honour must be shown to all, especially to those who share our faith [Ga 6:10] and to pilgrims.
>
> Once a guest has been announced, the Superior and the brothers are to meet him with all the courtesy of love. First of all, they are to pray together and thus be united in peace. Prayer must always precede the kiss of peace because of the delusions of the devil.
>
> All humility should be shown in addressing a guest on arrival or departure. By a bow of the head or by a complete prostration of the body, Christ is to be adored because he is indeed welcomed in them. After the guests have been received, they should be invited to pray; then the Superior or an appointed brother will sit with them. The divine law is read to the guest for his instruction, and after that every kindness is shown him. The Superior may break his fast for the sake of a guest, unless it is a day of special fast which cannot be broken. The brothers, however, observe the usual fast. The Abbot shall pour water on the hands of the guests. The Abbot with the entire community shall wash their feet. After the washing they will recite this

verse: 'God we have received your mercy in the midst of your temple' [Ps 48:9].

Great care and concern are to be shown in receiving poor people and pilgrims, because in them more particularly Christ is received; our very awe of the rich guarantees them special respect.

The kitchen for the abbot and guests ought to be separate, so that guests—and monasteries are never without them—need not disturb the brothers when they present themselves at unpredictable hours. Each year, two brothers who can do the work competently are to be assigned to this kitchen. Additional help should be available when needed so that they can perform this service without grumbling, on the other hand, when the work slackens, they are to go wherever other duties are assigned them. This consideration is not for them alone, but applies to all duties in the monastery; the brothers are to be given help when it is needed, and whenever they are free, they work wherever they are assigned.

The guest quarters are to be entrusted to a God-fearing brother. Adequate bedding should be available there. The house of God should be in the care of wise men who will manage it wisely.

No one is to speak or associate with guests unless he is bidden; however, if a brother meets or sees a guest, he is to greet him humbly, as we have said. He asks for a blessing and continues on his way, explaining that he is not allowed to speak with a guest.[3]

Monastic charity suffered under the Merovingian dynasty in Gaul but in the eighth century under Charlemagne church property was recovered, tithes were restored, and all the traditional charitable features of church life were revived, particularly the tradition of regarding the Church's possessions as the 'patrimony of the poor.' The bishop recovered his position as the supreme director of the administration of charity, and the monasteries were expected to maintain their ancient charitable work. The great monastic figures of England such as St Bede (c. 673–735) and Alcuin (c. 735–804) again taught that all superfluous wealth should go to the poor.

Deprived however of Charlemagne's all-embracing rule, much of the Church's charity declined, Christendom suffered a lack of cohesion, and the work of poor relief was gradually transferred from the bishops to the monasteries. This was because monasteries had become a more important concentration of Christian life, whereas the diocesan clergy were often demoralized and the parish poor suffered. Endowments were made more and more to monasteries rather than parishes; tenants of monasteries often found fairer treatment, and in general monasteries exercised a more stabilising influence. 'The energy of the Christian life had gone over from the diocese to the monastery.'[4]

Monasteries became centre for rich and poor alike, high and low, for innocent youth and repentant age. They provided in some measure a substitute for the primitive episcopal parish. In every district, alike on towering mountain and in lowly valley, monasteries arose which formed centres of the organized religious life for the neighbourhood, maintained schools, provided models for agriculture, industry, pisciculture and forestry, sheltered the traveller, relieved the poor, reared the orphans, cared for the sick, and were havens of refuge for all who were weighed down by spiritual or corporal misery. They became centres of all religious charitable and cultural activity.

The religious most prominent in the work of charity were the Benedictines, the Cistercians, the Premonstratensians, the Dominicans, and the Franciscans. The porters of the communities of these orders would distribute alms each day at the monastery or friary gate to the needy and would even call to assist the housebound. Many monasteries also ran hospices for the sick which together with their improvement of social conditions and better treatment of tenants and servants won them a new respect. The monasteries also ran schools where rich and poor were treated alike.

The message of St Francis (c. 1181–1226) recalled all the old Gospel idealism, with a chivalric interpretation; he taught holy poverty, revived the care of the social outcast and the leper, reclaimed many from a life of self-indulgent luxury, and gave immense impetus to the work of charity.

Cardinal Gasquet describes the hospitality of Benedictines to rich and poor alike.

> The guest-house (*hostellary, hostry,* etc.) was a necessary part of every great religious house. It was presided over by a senior monk, whose duty it was to keep the hall and chambers ready for the reception of guests, and to be ever prepared to receive those who came to ask for hospitality. Naturally the guest-house was situated where it would be least likely to interfere with the privacy of the monastery. The guest-place at Canterbury was of great size, measuring forty feet broad by a hundred and

fifty feet long. The main building was a big hall, resembling a church with columns, having on each side bedrooms or cubicles leading out of it. In the thirteenth century John de Hertford, abbot of St Alban's, built a noble hall for the use of guests frequenting his abbey, with an inner parlour having a fireplace in it, and many chambers arranged for the use of various kinds of guests. It had also a *pro-aula,* or reception-room, in which the guest-master first received the pilgrim or traveller, before conducting him to the church, or arranging for a reception corresponding to his rank and position.

In the greater monastic establishments there were frequently several places for the reception of guests. The abbot, or superior, had rooms to accommodate distinguished or honoured guests and benefactors of the establishment. The cellarer's department, too, frequently had to entertain merchants and others who came upon business of the house: a third shelter was provided near the gate of the monastery for the poorer folk, and a fourth for the monks of other religious houses, who had their meals in the common refectory, and joined in many of the exercises of the community.

The *Rites of Durham* thus describes the guest-house which the author remembered in the great cathedral monastery of the North:

'There was a famous house of hospitality, called the Guest Hall, within the Abbey garth of Durham, on the west side, towards the water, the Terrar of the house being master thereof, as one appointed to give entertainment to all states, both noble, gentle, and whatsoever degree that came thither as strangers, their entertainment not being inferior to any place in England, both for the goodness of their diet, the sweet and dainty furniture of their lodgings, and generally all things necessary for travellers. And, withal, this entertainment continuing, (the monks) not willing or commanding any man to depart, upon his honest and good behaviour. This hall is a goodly, brave place, much like unto the body of a church, with very fair pillars supporting it on either side, and in the midst of the hall a most large range for the fire. The chambers and lodgings belonging to it were sweetly kept and so richly furnished that they were not unpleasant to lie in, especially one chamber called the 'king's chamber,' deserving that name, in that the king himself might very well have lain in it, for the princely linen thereof … The prior (whose hospitality was such as that there needed no guest-hall, but that they (the Convent) were desirous to abound in all liberal and free almsgiving) did keep a most honourable house and very noble entertainment, being attended upon both with gentlemen and yeomen, of the best in the country, as the honourable service of his house deserved no less. The benevolence thereof, with the relief and alms of the whole Convent, was always open and free, not only to the poor of the city of Durham, but to all the poor people of the country besides.'

In most monastic statutes, the time during which a visitor was to be allowed free hospitality was not unlimited, as, according to the recollection of the author of the *Rites of Durham*, appears to have been the case in that monastery. The usual period was apparently two days and nights, and in ordinary cases after dinner on the third day the guest was expected to take his departure. If for any reason a visitor desired to prolong his stay, permission had to be obtained from the superior by the guest-master. Unless prevented by sickness, after that time the guest had to rise for Matins, and otherwise follow the exercises of the community. With the Franciscans, a visitor who asked for hospitality from the convent beyond three days, had to beg pardon in the conventual chapter before he departed for his excessive demand upon the hospitality of the house....

No religious house was complete without a place where the poor could come and beg alms in the name of Christ. The convent doles of food and clothing were administered by one of the senior monks, who, by his office of almoner, had to interview the crowds of poor who daily flocked to the gate in search of relief. His charity was to be wider than his means; and where he could not satisfy the actual needs of all, he was at least to manifest his Christian sympathy for their sufferings. The house or room, from which the monastic relief was given, frequently stood near the church, as showing the necessary connection between charity and religion. In most of the almonries, at any rate in those of the larger monasteries, there was a free school for poor boys. It was in these that most of the students who were presented for Ordination by the religious houses in such number during the fourteenth and fifteenth centuries, (as is shown by the episcopal registers of the English dioceses), were prepared to exercise their sacred ministry in the ranks of the parochial clergy.[5]

Monastic Hospitality

Lanfranc (c. 1005–89), archbishop of Canterbury, wrote in his Monastic Constitutions:

> The Almoner, either himself if occasion serve, or by means of reliable and truthful servants, shall take great pains to discover where may lie those sick and weakly persons who are without means of sustenance. If he himself goes forth to seek and visit the indigent, he shall take two servants with him, and before he enters the house to which he is going he shall cause any women who may be there to leave it. Entering the house he shall speak kindly and comfort the sick man and offer him the best of what he has that may be needful for him. If the sick man ask for something else he shall do what he can to obtain it. He shall never enter houses in which sick or infirm women are lying, but shall send to them all necessaries that he can by means of one of his servants. But before he gives any help of the kind mentioned above he shall tell the abbot or prior, and apportion the alms of the monastery according to their decision.[6]

Dr Moorman relates:

> At Durham we find considerable sums spent on bread for the poor, besides the purchase of boots and shoes for the same purpose. At Norwich the almoner disposed of cloth, shoes, ale, meat, fish, eggs, bread and peat. At Ramsey thirteen poor men were supported, each receiving daily 1 ½ loaves, half a gallon of beer, a dish of pottage and half a monk's ration of whatever was cooked in the kitchen. On fast-days each was to have three herrings for dinner and one for supper. They also received some cloth and either a pair of boots or 4d.

Many religious houses maintained a certain number of poor men actually within their walls. At Barnwell, for example, five poor men lived in the almonry together with some young clerks who were supported by the canons. The canons of Dunstable in 1272 took into their infirmary a blind clerk who remained there 'for a very long time' (*diutissime*), and seculars seem to have been looked after in the infirmaries of a number of Cistercian abbeys, including Waverley, Pipewell, Meaux and Newminster. At Fountains, towards the end of the twelfth century, during a time of plague, the poor flocked to the abbey and tents had to be erected to accommodate them, both lay nurses and priests being provided by the monks to care for the sick. Bermondsey, which was found to be dispensing alms in a perfectly satisfactory way in 1262 when inspected by the Cluniac visitors, had a hospital built in 1213 for converts from the Jewish faith and for poor boys.

Gilbertine houses also had hostels attached for the care of the poor and the sick, lepers and orphans. Feasts in the monasteries to which the poor were invited were also common, in addition to the regular distribution of gifts on Maundy Thursday. Poor were fed in the hall at Norwich; at Winchcombe 100 poor people were to be fed on the morrow of All Saints; at Butley in Suffolk the poor were fed seven times a year; and at Newminster, on St Katharine's Day, 100 poor persons were to receive two oatcakes and two herrings each. At Evesham thirty poor were fed once a year in the parlour on the anniversary of the death of Prior Thomas. Several individual abbots and priors were noted for the generosity of their almsgiving: Hugh of

Durham, for example, was so popular that when he was returning home the poor would flock to meet him and conduct him to the priory with singing.[7]

Thus monastic charity won the thirteenth century Church an unequalled reputation.

Notes

[1] H. Waddell, *The Desert Fathers* (London, Constable, 1936), XIII, 2–13 (p. 155). For a general account of Egyptian monasticism at this period, see L. Duchesne, *Early History of the Christian Church, from its Foundation until the End of the Fifth Century*, 3 vols. (London, John Murray, 1909–24), vol. ii, pp. 386–413.

[2] Possidius, *Life of St Augustine*, XXV, from *Sancti Augustini Vita ... ed. with rev. text, introduction, notes, and an English version* by Herbert T. Weiskotten (Princeton, Princeton University Press, 1919). See also Peter Brown, *Augustine of Hippo* (London, Faber & Faber, 1967), p. 198.

[3] *The Rule of St Benedict in English*, ed T. Fry (Collegeville, Minnesota, The Liturgical Press, 1981), ch. 53 — The Reception of Guests. This chapter of course applies to all guests but should have special application to the needy.

[4] G. Ratzinger, *Der Geschichte Kirchlichen Armenpflege* (Freiburg, Freiburg Univ., 1884), pp. 287–288.

[5] F. A. Gasquet, *English Monastic Life* (London, Methuen and Co, 1906), pp. 30–33. For *The Rites of Durham*, see J. T. Fowler (ed.), *The Rites of Durham, being a description or brief declaration of all the ancient monuments, rites and customs belonging or being within the monastical church of Durham before the suppression, written 1593* (Durham, Surtees Society vol. cvii, 1902).

[6] *The Monastic Constitutions of Lanfranc*, trans. D. Knowles (Oxford, Oxford University Press, 1951), pp. 88–89. Knowles comments, 'The function of the almoner as a district visitor seems to have ceased early in England, and alms were distributed at the gateway or in the almonry.'

[7] J. R. H. Moorman, *Church Life in England in the Thirteenth Century* (Cambridge, Cambridge University Press, 1945), pp.

358–359. For a survey of comparable developments on the continent from the fifth to the eleventh century, see Mollat, M., *The Poor in the Middle Ages: An Essay in Social History*, trans. from the French by A. Goldhammer (New Haven and London, Yale University Press, 1986), pp. 13–113.

CHAPTER 6

Hospitals and Hospitallers

Hospices for pilgrims and wayfarers in Merovingian Gaul were quite numerous in the seventh century and were largely served by monasteries. St Benedict had instructed his monks to care for the sick as well as the stranger, but in practice while monasteries gave the poor traveller hospitality, their infirmaries catered only for the monks themselves.

The custom of the early Church, of bishops using their property to house the poor, continued in part, particularly where there was eastern influence such as in Clermont and Poitou. The hospice in Poitou was founded by Bishop Praeiectus of Auvergne (c. 600–676) who no doubt had contact with Eastern merchants in his diocese and whose chronicler uses the Greek word *xenodochion* to describe his foundation, adding that Praeiectus followed 'the customs of the orientals.'[1] This foundation and other *xenodochia*, notably in Spain and in Rome, probably had medical facilities as a result of Greek influence.

The advent of Charlemagne saw a decline in Byzantine influence on the West and many *xenodochia* became redundant or fell to monasteries whose traditional hospitality did not always extend to prolonged care of the sick poor and who thus frequently abandoned them. A new word came to be applied in the West to describe houses for the poor traveller, who invariably was in need of some medical attention. The word *hospitale* implied a place of hospitality and had a more distinct meaning than the modern understanding of 'hospital'. A 'hospitaller' was one who administered hospitality and in this primitive context such work was of a similar character to Mother Teresa's Missionaries of Charity. The hospitals were not places for the care of the sick, but places of hospitality for the sick and poor alike.

The Latin word *hospes* means a guest, thus *hospitalia*, *hospitium*, hospice, hospital, and hostel all derive their meaning from a place of hospitality; these followed the original shelters known in the early church as *xenodochia* or *ptochotrophia* (homes for strangers and the poor) and presumably provided some medical attention. St Basil established one of the earliest of such institutions in the fourth century at the gates of Caesarea which gave rise to a new town exclusively concerned with those in need. St Gregory of Nazianzen (329–389) described it thus:

> Go forth a little way from the city, and behold the new city, the storehouse of piety, the common treasury of the wealthy ... where disease is regarded in a religious light, and disaster is thought a blessing, and sympathy is put to the test ... There is no longer before our eyes that terrible and piteous spectacle of men who are living corpses, the greater part of whose limbs have mortified, driven away from their cities and homes and public places and fountains, aye, and from their own dearest ones, recognizable by their names rather than by their features: they are no longer brought before us at our gatherings and meetings, in our common intercourse and union, no longer the objects of hatred, instead of pity on account of their disease; composers of piteous songs, if any of

them have their voice still left to them. [Basil] however it was, who took the lead in pressing upon those who were men, that they ought not to despise their fellowmen, nor to dishonour Christ, the one Head of all, by their inhuman treatment of them; but to use the misfortunes of others as an opportunity of firmly establishing their own lot, and to lend to God that mercy of which they stand in need at His hands. He did not therefore disdain to honour with his lips this disease, noble and of noble ancestry and brilliant reputation though he was, but saluted them as brethren, not, as some might suppose, from vainglory, (for who was so far removed from this feeling?) but taking the lead in approaching to tend them, as a consequence of his philosophy, and so giving not only a speaking, but also a silent, instruction ... Others have had their cooks, and splendid tables, and the devices and dainties of confectioners, and exquisite carriages, and soft, flowing robes; Basil's care was for the sick, and the relief of their wounds, and the imitation of Christ, by cleansing leprosy, not by a word, but in deed.[2]

This example was followed by similar foundations at Alexandria and Ephesus. The origins of such institutions are, it seems, to be found in the East. During the fourth century there was a shift in the monastic tradition from large monasteries in the countryside to smaller urban communities or *synoikiai*. This development, under the influence of Eustathius of Sabasteia (c. 300–c. 377), inspired the foundation of houses of charity for the urban poor. This same Eustathius was to influence both Patriarch Macedonius (d. 362) at Constantinople and St Basil at Caesarea in their setting up of ecclesiastical establishments to help the poor.

Unfortunately Eustathius and Macedonius, and indeed the whole movement of fourth century urban philanthropy, became linked with heresy.[3] Consequently St Basil's foundation at Caesarea, through its unwavering orthodoxy, came to represent a more acceptable application of Christian charity; St John Chrysostom moreover, when founding hospitals at Constantinople c. 400, incorporated them within the ecclesiastical structure. Palladius describes his work thus,

> As the need of treatment was very great, he erected other hospitals, over which he appointed two devout priests, as well as doctors and cooks, and kindly workers from among his celibates to assist them; so that strangers coming to the city, and there falling ill, could obtain medical care, as a thing which was not only good in itself, but also for the glory of the Saviour.[4]

These early Eastern infirmaries therefore were often hospitals in the modern sense in addition to being a refuge for the poor. Perhaps the earliest such institution exclusively concerned with medical treatment was the *xenodochion* of St Sampson at Constantinople which had a resident staff of surgeons.

The word *xenodochion* was a generic description for such institutions for sick or poor, although it means literally a shelter for strangers; 'infirmary' in the West became the distinctive title for places of medical care before 'hospital' came to embrace the same meaning and so lost its original association with the hospitality of the Church.

Although the East witnessed the pioneering of hospitaller movements, the first public hospital in Rome was established by one Fabiola of the house of the Fabii as early as 390 under the guidance of St Jerome (c. 342–420) who called it a *nosocomium*, indicating that it was for the sick and helpless poor.[5] Paula, another associate of St Jerome, set up pilgrim hospices on the road to Bethlehem and a hospital in Jerusalem.[6] St Theodosius (423–529) opened two medical centres near Jerusalem.[7] In York in 947 the cathedral canons founded the Hospital of St Peter, which must be the earliest in Britain and as with other such early establishments was most likely a hostel, which gave hospitality to strangers and pilgrims.[8]

The Order of the Hospitallers arose after the end of the persecution of Christians under the Egyptian Caliph Al-Hakim (985–1021), when pilgrim traffic to the Holy Land began to increase. Merchants from Amalfi, who were trading with Jerusalem, sought to restore the old Latin monastery and hospice of Our Lady of the Latins at Jerusalem, as we are told by William of Tyre (c. 1130–c. 1185), archbishop of Tyre and chancellor of the Kingdom of Jerusalem, in his *History of Deeds Done Beyond the Sea*. When they had done this, they introduced a congregation of Italian Benedictines who gave shelter to the merchants in the hospice when on business or visiting the shrines in Jerusalem. The merchants also founded a convent of nuns to run a hospice for women and later, with the influx of poor pilgrims and travellers, they founded a third hospice for homeless wayfarers.

The merchants entrusted this third hospice to the care of lay brothers who were to become perhaps the first hospitaller community from the West. The hospice's warden was appointed by the Abbot of St Mary of the Latins until the Crusaders took Jerusalem in 1099, following a siege in which the warden known to posterity as 'Blessed Gerard' (d. 1120) gave invaluable assistance to the Christian army.[9] Gerard, no doubt using the influence he had recently obtained, now succeeded in winning for the hospital independence from the presiding Abbot, as we learn from the writings of Amato of Monte Cassino, in archaeological evidence, and from the Bull *Pie Postulatio Voluntatis* of 15th February 1113 confirming the thirteen-year-old Order.[10]

Pie Postulatio Voluntatis describes the hospice as 'the *Xenodocheum*, ... founded in the City of Jerusalem, near to the Church of the Blessed John the Baptist,' and it refers to other hospices which Gerard governed in the west as *Xenodochea* or *Ptochea*. The lay brothers saw their labours in caring for poor travellers as the practice of Christian virtue and as an integral part of a religious life in which the care of those in their charge included the provision of prayer and the sacraments; thus at the great hospital in Jerusalem great stress was laid on the importance of prayer, and the Rule of Gerard's successor, Fra' Raymond du Puy (Master 1120 – c. 1160),[11] ordained:

> when the sick man shall come there, let him be received thus, let him partake of the Holy Sacrament, first having confessed his sins to the priest, and afterwards let him be carried to bed, and there as if he were a Lord, each day before the brethren go to eat, let him be refreshed with food charitably according to the ability of the House.

The Order taught the same divine economy that the early Church had taught: the rich by giving alms to Christ in the poor, atoned for sin while the poor, receiving benefits as if from God, but through human agency, prayed for the donor. The rich thus gave charity in kind and the poor in spirit. This spirit of the Hospital created a more godly vocation than that of arms and in reviving the early Church's service and hospitality to the poor, but with a renewed romantic vision, introduced a new element to the religious movements of Christendom. The eastern monks had pioneered a different kind of hospital manned by lay staff, to which the Order had made important adaptations for the West, where monks had not made the same commitment to public infirmaries. The Hospitallers' new vision may even have spread to long-established institutions: by the Mastership of Fra' Roger there was a Hospitaller Prior of Constantinople who had under him the old Sampson Xenon which had played a seminal role in the development of the Byzantine hospital.[12]

The community came to be called the Brethren of the Hospital (*domus hospitalis*) of Jerusalem and by the end of the twelfth century the brothers had developed their work to include an infirmary for the sick, thus going beyond the work of the Benedictines whose care of the sick was largely restricted to the monks of their own Order. The Hospitallers, as they came to be known, thus brought to the West the example of the Christian infirmaries in the East, but with the difference that the infirmaries were run by brethren living under a monastic rule, the Rule of St Augustine. By developing a medical role separate from the giving of refuge to poor travellers, the Hospitallers gave a new meaning to the word *hospital*, which came to embrace the meaning of infirmary. This composite function of service to sick and poor alike, under the care of such dedicated brethren, inspired the West to show a renewed Christian zeal in the corporal works of mercy and to establish many similar institutions, modelled on the Hospital of St John of Jerusalem.

The Church in the West was already taking active steps to accommodate the poor in what were new and changed conditions. Urban development had taken men away from the land and brought widespread poverty, disease, and insanitary conditions to the now crowded cities. Robert of Arbrissel (c. 1046–1116), founder of Fontevrault Abbey and a monk with a social conscience, worked strenuously for the poor and sick. Radulf of Ardens (died c. 1200) went so far as to compare all poor men with Lazarus in Christ's parable, and the rich with Dives, who was condemned to suffer want in the life to come. However the hospitals of the day were still ecclesiastical rather than medical institutions, providing care rather than cure, and bodily refreshment was secondary to the salvation of the soul. Thus the routines of pilgrim hospices, hospitals for the homeless traveller, and infirmaries for the poor sick were punctuated by religious observances to strengthen faith. Life was short and often miserable for the poor with no material prospects, so as bodily infirmity took its hold the inmates were encouraged to prepare for the life to come. Spiritual care apart from the material necessities of life was the main ingredient of such foundations, with the result that even if medical science was absent, faith and love prevailed.

Augustinian canons were among the first religious to appreciate the need for a more practical interpretation of the Gospel in public philanthropy in the twelfth century. They established new canonries to minister to larger urban populations, departing from the old traditional Cathedral Chapters and the distant life of personal asceticism. Similar new communities came into existence, including the Antonines, the Trinitarians, and the Premonstratensians; while the Rule of St Augustine provided a framework for lay communities such as the Hospitaller Order of St John of Jerusalem. These communities revived public philanthropy in France and Germany where more ancient foundations had sunk into decay.

In England Rahere, a former court jester, established St Bartholomew's in London, the first English hospital in the modern sense, in 1123. St Bartholomew's was served by Augustinian canons and Rahere became their first prior. He had been taken with malaria while a pilgrim in Rome and had been nursed by the Canons of St Bartholomew on the Tiber. He vowed, if he recovered, to found a similar hospital in England.

Medical treatment in the early days at St Bartholomew's sometimes relied on faith, such as when a woman with a swollen tongue was brought to Prior Rahere and he dipped a relic of the cross in water, wished her better, and painted a cross on her tongue. For the most part no records survive of the various ailments and the treatment given, except in the case of miracles, for instance the woman with the swollen tongue returned home 'gladde and hole.'[13] The fourteenth century saw greater sophistication with the publication of the *Breviarium Bartholomei* (1381) in which olive oil is recommended for rheumatism, with heated oil being applied to the affected area, all being done within a formula of prayer which may have been as much a timing device as a spiritual remedy. In general note was taken of diet and the condition of a patient's water was shown to the physician, which suggests a conscientious if primitive medical care.

Although most of the hospices reorganized by the Augustinians simply expanded the original provision of food and shelter to the poor, many came to follow the example of the Hospital at Jerusalem and concentrate on the treatment of the sick poor as well. The twelfth century therefore saw the rise of Augustinian lay brotherhoods dedicated to the corporal works of mercy in a renewed Christian commitment to the poor. Some brotherhoods such as the Alexian Brothers became canonically established as religious communities. This became so extensive that in England alone there were over 750 functioning hospices and hospitals[14] for a population of less than 4,000,000, while about 1,500 monasteries still gave food and shelter to wayfarers. Public charity was thus provided for all, medically unsophisticated but done, at its best, in a spirit of Christian love. This was a truly conscientious effort to serve Christ in the poor and proves the value of private benevolence in caring for the poor and sick, as most of these hospitals were privately funded by local benefactors who turned to the Church and its religious orders to carry out their wishes.

Apart from the hospices for the wayfarers, pilgrims, the destitute and the infirm, there were many hospitals for lepers. These unfortunates were rendered homeless through their sickness, and their hospitals were usually isolated from the nearest township. One of the earliest in England was founded by Archbishop Lanfranc at Harbledown, near Canterbury, and could accommodate a hundred at a time; while one of the largest was St Leonard's York, which accommodated over two hundred sick and poor and ran a children's hospital for twenty-three boys. On the staff were bakers, brewers, carters, cooks, smiths, boatmen, a ferry woman, sixteen male and female servants, and a *hus-wyf*, presumably some a sort of matron.

Admittance to such hospitals was dependent on the consent of other residents, thus ensuring some degree of peaceful co-existence. In the case of a leper a sum of money would be given, and the candidate would swear an oath. The form of oath used at Buckland Hospital in Dover, which was run by the monks of Dover Priory, is preserved in the hospital's Register:

> I, — —, do promise before God and St Bartholomew and all saints, that to the best of my power I will be faithful and useful to the hospital, ... to be obedient to my superior and have love to my brethren and sisters. I will be sober and chaste of body; and a moiety of the goods I shall die possessed of, shall belong to the house. I will pray for the peace of the church and the realm of England, and for the king and queen, and for the prior and convent of St Martin, and for the burgesses of Dover on sea and land, and especially for all our benefactors, living and dead.[15]

The applicant was then sprinkled with holy water and escorted to the altar where he knelt to receive the warden's blessing. He was bound to the daily recitation of two hundred *Pater Nosters* and *Aves* and each night a bell would ring to signal the recitation of the same sitting upright in bed.

The master or warden of most hospitals was appointed by the patron, but in some of them he was elected by the staff. At St John's Hospital, Oxford, founded in 1213 for strangers and the infirm, the master was chosen by the staff from among the three Augustinian chaplains, who with six lay brothers and six lay sisters made up the staff of the various artisans and husbandmen. The master of a hospital was often forbidden hunting, card playing and hand ball; he could not visit ale houses or leave the hospital overnight. The chaplain of the hospital at Wells was similarly expected to be 'circumspect and expert in spiritual and temporal things, and free from all infamous vice.'[16]

Not all the brethren were employed in caring for the residents: a proctor was usually allocated to collect alms, for the hospitals were largely dependent on charity, though some received regular donations from their patrons or derived rents from land or property. Some hospitals held an annual fair by royal charter to raise money, or extracted tolls from local produce. At Carlisle, for instance, all residents of the hospital received a pot of ale and a loaf every Sunday from the brewers and bakers of the town.

The rules of the hospitals invariably required a weekly meeting to correct any infringements; punishments ranged from fines to fasting or even a flogging. Food was usually simple but plentiful: at Sherburn, Co Durham, for instance, each resident received a loaf and a gallon of beer daily, meat was had three times a week and on meatless days there were always vegetables, eggs and cheese. Beds for the most part were pallets of straw, but by the end of the twelfth century these were complemented with substantial wooden bedsteads, which invariably had to accommodate two or more at a time. The Hospitallers of St John of Jerusalem were the first to pioneer one to a bed and provide regular clean linen, although we do not know how often bed linen was changed. St Thomas's Hospital, Canterbury, made an annual payment of 46s. 8d. 'to

Rauf Cokker keper of the seid hospitall and his wif for kepyng wasshyng of the bedds for poure people.'[17] Each new resident usually received clean sheets.

Apart from the destitute, the pilgrims, and the sick, there were also almshouses for the aged poor and hostels for the insane, unmarried mothers, poor clergy, lay gentlefolk, orphans, converts, and Jews. Pilgrim hospices greatly increased after 1170 with the mass of poor pilgrims, wayfarers and sick seeking a remedy at the shrine of St Thomas of Canterbury. Hospitals dedicated to St Thomas were established at Canterbury and Southwark (the forerunner of the modern London hospital) and poor English pilgrims in Rome were also accommodated in a hospital dedicated to the 'blissful martyr.' Apart from the Hospitallers of St John, other military orders concerned themselves with hospital management: the Order of St Mary of Bethlehem, the Order of St Anthony of Vienne, and the Hospitaller Order of St Thomas of Acre, which was founded during the Third Crusade to nurse English crusaders in the Holy Land and in their London hospital on Cheapside, and also cared for London's sick and poor. The Order of St Lazarus of Jerusalem was dedicated to nursing lepers and had its principal English hospital at Burton Lazars in Leicestershire. However after the middle of the fourteenth century, when leprosy declined in England, many leper hospitals turned to catering for the poor and sick in general.

Episcopal patronage of hostels for the homeless remained a continuing tradition, ever since the days of the early Church when the bishops had been called 'Fathers of the Poor'. In the Exeter Pontifical and in the Sarum liturgical tradition each bishop at his consecration was asked 'will you show mercy and kindness, for the name of the Lord, to the poor, the stranger, and all in want?' In the current Roman Pontifical, the candidate is asked: 'Are you resolved to show kindness and compassion in the name of the Lord, to the poor and to the stranger and to all who are in any need?' The candidate is later asked to 'love the poor and infirm, strangers and the homeless.' Among these early 'Fathers of the Poor,' who must be considered not only the first patrons, but also among the earliest pioneers, of hospitals for the poor, were St Clement, St Cyprian, St Basil the Great, St Gregory of Nazianzen and St John Chrysostom. In some cases this episcopal obligation of hospitality came to be fulfilled not by the bishop in person, but by religious communities, whose vocation was to serve the poor and who often followed the Rule of St Augustine, and who included Hospitallers and occasionally Franciscans.

Notes

1. T. Miller, 'The Knights of St John and the Hospitals of the Latin West,' *Speculum* vol. 53, 1978, pp. 710–711.
2. St Gregory's Oration XLIII (the Funeral Oration on St Basil), 63, trans. C. G. Browne & J. G. Swallow, in *St Cyril of Jerusalem and St Gregory of Nazianzen*, Select Library of Nicene and Post-Nicene Fathers, series 2, vol. 7, ed. P. Schaff & H. Wace (Oxford, James Parker & Co, 1894).
3. T. Miller, p. 723.
4. Palladius, *Dialogue*, 135, from *Dialogue concerning the Life of St John Chrysostom*, trans. H. Moore (London, 1921). Quoted in J. J. Walsh, *The Catholic Church and Healing* (London, Burns Oates and Washbourne Ltd, 1928), p. 21.
5. St Jerome, Letter 77.6.
6. J. J. Walsh, p. 22.
7. T. Miller, p. 727.
8. J. Woodward, *To Do the Sick No Harm — A Study of the British*

Voluntary Hospital System to 1875 (London, Routledge Keegan & Paul, 1974), p. 1.

9   Gerard used to throw loaves to the starving Christian besiegers, but when he was arrested and called before the Arab governor, the loaves miraculously turned into stones. See J. Riley-Smith, *The Knights of St John of Jerusalem and Cyprus* (London, Macmillan, 1967), pp. 37–38.
10 Translation in E. J. King, pp. 16–19.
11 Translation *ibid.*, pp. 20–28.
12 *ibid.*, p. 37 n. 5. The brethren and inmates of this Hospital were massacred by a mob in 1183, and the Priory of Constantinople subsequently ceased to exist.
13 Quoted *ibid.*, p. 95.
14 Nearly 800 are listed in R. M. Clay, *The Mediaeval Hospitals of England* (London, Frank Cass & Co Ltd, 1966), pp. 277–337. More recent identifications have taken the number up to 980.
15 Quoted *ibid.*, p. 131, from the register of St Bartholomew's, Dover.
16 Quoted *ibid.*, p. 151.
17 Quoted *ibid.*, p. 173.

CHAPTER 7

OUR LORDS THE POOR

CHANGES IN RELIGIOUS practice and the inspiration of the day in the late eleventh and early twelfth centuries favoured a more practical expression of the Catholic faith which gave rise to a new movement in Christendom. Part of this new movement were the military and religious orders, of which the Hospitallers proved perhaps the most successful. The survival of the Hospitallers was in part due to their dual role as fighting men and carers for the sick and poor. Their origins in eleventh century Jerusalem were purely philanthropic as indicated in the epitaph of Blessed Gerard the founder, 'the most humble man in the East and the servant of the poor.'[1] These words indicate the calling he wished to instil in his brethren, and in corroboration William of Tyre says that he 'long rendered service to the poor.'[2] *Pie Postulatio Voluntatis* raised the brethren of the Hospital to the dignity of a religious order and for many years they provided care and shelter at their hospital in Jerusalem. They became a military order of chivalry but unlike the Templars could escape some of the opprobrium levelled at the purely military orders by reverting to their philanthropic ministry.

Blessed Gerard's successor, Fra' Raymond du Puy, replaced the hospital's Benedictine tradition with the adaptable Rule of St Augustine which became a characteristic of most Hospitaller communities like the Knights of St Lazarus and those of St Thomas of Acre. This Rule more adequately facilitated the corporal works of mercy and the chivalric ideal, and bade the brethren treat the poor as their Lords. The care of these liege Lords remained at the heart of the Order and new brethren were instructed to regard the sick and poor as their Lords. Thus those received into their care were addressed as, 'My Lords the sick,' and, 'My Lords the poor,' and were given great deference.

Hospitallers laboured personally in the hospital, and did not delegate the work to lay staff. Fra' Raymond described himself as 'Servant of Christ's Poor and Warden of the Hospital of Jerusalem'; while the Statutes of Fra' Roger des Moulins (Master 1177–87)[3] direct that, 'guarding and watching them day and night, the brethren of the Hospital should serve the sick poor with zeal and devotion as if they were their Lords.' The spirituality of the Order, in which the code of service to a liege Lord was spiritualized to strengthen the Hospitaller vocation, was quite distinct from anything in the Byzantine tradition. The brethren were to show faithful service as serfs to their Lords the sick and poor; Fra' Raymond claimed in a letter to bishops in the West that his Hospitallers were 'as sure of receiving the Mercy of Christ as those who went on crusade.'[4] The feudal virtues were thus spiritualized and the Hospitaller vocation as the better part of chivalry remains as relevant today as in the twelfth century.

St Francis of Assisi was to put this dedication to the poor and sick into the context of a spiritualized form of chivalry, for he reinvented the chivalric code using its language to describe a romantic understanding of a radical Gospel life. This had surely been anticipated in the ideals of the Order, and when the Hopitallers declared themselves serfs in the service of their Lords the sick such spiritual refinement must have touched the heart of the young Francis.[5]

Documentary evidence survives from the twelfth century of the care at the great Hospital at Jerusalem.[6] Much greater stress was laid on comfort and diet than on the role of the physician, no doubt reflecting contemporary medical science. Thus the Rule of Fra' Raymond had required the brethren to feed the sick before they themselves ate;[7] and the diet of the sick was comparable with that of the wealthier classes: the Statutes of Fra' Jobert (Grand Master 1172–7)[8] required the sick to be given the luxury of white bread; and the Statutes of Fra' Roger noted that, 'for three days in the week the sick are accustomed to have fresh meat, either pork or mutton, and those who are unable to eat it have chicken.'[9]

The Hospital could hold up to 2,000, as we are told by John of Würzburg, who visited it in the 1160s, and the brethren fed an equal number of poor on a daily basis. If the medical side was somewhat sparse compared to a modern infirmary, we must remember that a hospital at this time was literally a place of hospitality. Thus what the Hospital provided was largely food, shelter, rest, and recuperation. Each of the Hospital's eleven wards was staffed by twelve Hospitallers, comprising a master and eleven assistants, but their task was palliative rather than medical.

John of Würzburg noted matter-of-factly that there were fifty deaths a day. The bed spaces were immediately filled, which indicates the great need for such an institution. The mortality rate, despite being rather shocking by modern standards, indicates the role of hospitals of the time, which was simply to give shelter, food, and comfort, rather than prescribe remedies, somewhat on a par with the modern 'hospice' where the terminally ill are given comfort and support in their last days.

The Statutes of Fra' Roger required that

> there should be engaged four wise doctors, who are qualified to examine urine, and to diagnose different diseases, and are able to administer appropriate medicines ... each bed should be covered with its own coverlet, and each bed should have its own special sheets ... each of the sick should have a cloak of sheepskin and boots for going to and coming from the latrines, and caps of wool ... little cradles should be made for the babies of the women pilgrims born in the House, so that they may lie separate, and that the baby in its own bed may be in no danger from the restlessness of its mother ... in every ward and place in the hospital, nine serjeants should be kept at their service, who should wash their feet gently, and change their sheets, and make their beds, and administer to the weak necessary and strengthening food ...[10]

Pope Lucius III, c. 1184, insisted that there should be a minimum of five physicians and three surgeons on duty in the Hospital, a reasonable number for the standards of western Europe but a paltry number compared to the hospitals of Byzantium and the Islamic world.

The Hospital would admit any in need of care including poor wayfarers, notwithstanding that most residents were Christian pilgrims. People of all faiths were admitted, a substantial number being those who had been injured in conflict and had been recovered by the Order's field-hospital unit. When all the beds were occupied the brethren would give up their own beds to sleep on the floor.

Considering the primitive conditions of the times the Hospital was remarkably sophisticated. Men and women had separate wards and each patient had a separate bed. There was also a maternity section in which if the mothers could not cope for their babies the Order would pay wet nurses to care for them. The Hospital also had a section for foundlings and orphans and required the wet nurses to regularly bring their charges to the Hospital for checkups, and if they failed in their duties others would be found to replace them.

Thus apart from the sick and the poor the Hospital had a number of youthful residents who when of age might decide either to join the Order as a serving brother or make their own way in the world. The Order expected catholics in their care to take part in the Order's religious life: they made their confession on admission and received Holy Communion before they were given a bed. In the main ward there was an altar where daily Mass was offered and this was considered an essential part of the spiritual care and comfort of the Hospital.

The Order had many properties that were called hospitals but this often expressed an association rather than a practical function: many gave shelter to poor and sick travellers but only the great hospitals such as those at Compostella, Genoa, Bargota, and Jerusalem had an infirmary to provide some measure of medical care. Several leper hospitals were also placed under the care of the Order.

The hospitaller and military roles of the knights were originally linked, and at first all military activity was exclusively connected with the protection and defence of pilgrims; however under Fra' Raymond the military role became extended to the defence of the Faith. The Order's maxim, *Obsequium Pauperum* (the Service of the Poor), was thus supplemented by *Tuitio Fidei* (Defence of the Faith), which came to be of equal importance. The ideal of chivalry perhaps finds its most romantic expression in the Hospitaller vocation particularly when expressed as 'the honour of God, courtesy to all and service to Christ in the sick and the poor.'[11]

In 1187 after the Battle of Hattin the Order lost Jerusalem and the use of its Hospital, but pilgrims continued to be housed in the stables of the old hospital just north of St Stephen's Gate and the Order moved its headquarters to Acre, where a hospital had existed since 1155. By 1191 the Hospitallers had considerably extended this new operational centre. Women continued to be treated at the main hospital but the Hospitaller Sisters moved out into their own convent of St Mary Magdalen. The code of the hospital ensured that all would be received and it is said that even Saladin visited the hospital to test this reputation of magnanimity. The Emperor Frederick II recovered Jerusalem in 1229 and the brethren moved back to their old hospital, but in 1244 the city fell once more, this time to the Turks.

In 1291 even Acre fell to the Moslems and the Order moved its headquarters to Limassol on the island of Cyprus, where they planned to build another hospital; however after the conquest of Rhodes in 1306 these plans were suspended and by 1314 the new hospital had been built at Collachium on Rhodes. The Order's priorities now changed, and there was a definite shift towards treatment of the sick rather than accommodation of the poor. The new hospital continued to give hospitality to pilgrims but medical nursing, particularly of the brethren of the Order injured in battle, took priority. There were also isolation wards for certain infectious diseases, a great advance for the time. A dramatic change had taken place, for the hospital at Jerusalem had received anyone who asked, including Moslems, Jews, and Greek and Latin Christians, whereas there is little evidence that this magnanimity continued on Rhodes.

The new hospital was enlarged by Fra' Antoni Fluvian de Riviere (Grand Master 1421–37). Each bed had its own cubicle and privy, ensuring the privacy of the sick, and patients dined off silver plates and drank from silver goblets. This level of treatment indicates the seriousness with which the Order regarded its ideal of treating the sick as Lords, but given the antiseptic character of silver it had a hygienic purpose as well. Physicians visited the patients twice a day and the Overseer would visit all the wards at Compline and Lauds to keep up patients' morale. A chapel and a refectory adjoined the wards and Mass was said daily in the great ward, though noble patients had private rooms on the first floor. The Prior and the Chaplain officiated at the daily Mass, heard confessions, and took Holy Communion to the bed-ridden.

The Order also had the privilege of burying criminals and lepers but their principle charge was the care of poor travellers, in furtherance of which the Order had hospitals at Genoa, a major staging post for pilgrims, and on the pilgrim route to Santiago de Compostela.

The Ottoman Turks saw the Order as a hindrance to their sea trade and besieged Rhodes in 1480, but without success. Finally in 1523 after a long struggle Suleiman the Magnificent forced the Order out of Rhodes, but out of respect for the knights' bravery and to save further loss of life, allowed them to depart with all their weaponry and with their honour intact. Shortly afterwards, in 1530, the Emperor Charles V gave the Order a new home on Malta.

Notes

1. Fulcher of Chartres, *Historia Hierosolymitana*, III, p. 446 sub anno 1120, quoted in H. J. A. Sire, *The Knights of Malta* (Newhaven & London, Yale Univ Press, 1994), p. 6.
2. William of Tyre, *Historia Rerum in Partibus Transmarinis Gestarum*, VII, 23, quoted in H. J. A. Sire, p. 209.
3. Translation *ibid.*, pp. 34–40.
4. Quoted by T. Miller, p. 732.
5. St Francis' redemption of the ideal of chivalry is described in more detail in *Gospel Chivalry: Franciscan Romanticism*, by Mark of Whitstable (Gracewing, Leominster, 2006), pp. 51–57.
6. For details, see H. Nicholson, *The Knights Hospitaller* (Woodbridge, Boydell Press, 2001), pp. 88–89, and H. J. A. Sire, p. 211.
7. See above, p. 37.
8. E. J. King, pp. 29–30.
9. *Ibid.*, p. 38.
10. *Ibid*, pp. 35–38.
11. Compare the Knight's Blessing: 'May Almighty God bless us and strengthen us in His service that we may honor Him, show courtesy to all, protect the weak and serve Christ in the sick and the poor. We ask this through Christ, Our Lord. Amen' (traditional, printed in *Journal of the Sovereign Military and Hospitaller Order of St John of Jerusalem of Rhodes and of Malta — Western Association U.S.A.* Volume 16.2 Autumn 2004, p. 15).

Chapter 8

The Mediaeval Poor Law[1]

THE MEDIAEVAL Church made laws, levied taxes, maintained courts, and paralleled the secular government in many ways, being the essential legal authority in much of everyday existence. As the relief of the poor was a precept of Christian charity the Church rightly claimed their care and protection, to which end she made special provision in canon law, her own body of law. The secular powers were often at odds with a universally acknowledged authority that did not come under their purview but canon law was to became the exclusive authority covering the relief of poverty.

As Europe emerged from the Dark Ages, old Roman law, as codified by Justinian, was re-discovered, but meanwhile the Church's accumulation of papal decrees, conciliar directives, and patristic tenets had become an embarrassing muddle. Gratian, a monk of Bologna, systematized all this heterogeneous material in 1140 in his *Decretum*. To this work were added further subsequent volumes, which covered new legislation, each with its own commentary or *Glossa Ordinaria*, all of which together made up what came to be known as the *Corpus Juris Canonici*. Gratian's work contains a large portion of the material relating to poor relief, mostly taken from early writings of the Fathers.[2]

The canonists' showed their concern for the poor by exempting them from court fees, a measure often considered characteristic of modern enlightenment.

Pope Honorius III in the thirteenth century went further, insisting that the poor should have counsel supplied free by the courts. The Church courts were moreover concerned to protect orphans and widows, in accordance with Exodus 22:22, and Gratian, following the tradition of the early Church, states: 'The bishop ought to be solicitous and vigilant concerning the defence of the poor and the relief of the oppressed.'[3]

The mediaeval poor law, as distinct from later counterparts, was founded on Biblical admonitions such as Ex 22:21; Mk 12:31; Lk 6:31; and Mt 25:34–40; and sought to exemplify Christian faith and to promote the seven corporal works of mercy. Moreover much of mediaeval teaching on poor relief had its basis in the family; after God all men should love first their families and then the stranger at their gate, and so poor relief was a general responsibility and by no means the exclusive duty of the bishops, clergy, and religious houses.

The Church did not ignore the spiritual rewards for acts of charity but emphasised the higher motive of the love of neighbour for his own sake. Mediaeval canonists were thus as concerned for the benefactor and the merit he or she gained as for the recipient, whereas modern legislators are largely concerned with recipients and their material welfare. In this church law makes the spiritual framework of charity paramount: the giver gives as to Christ, and the receiver receives as from God: 'Give, and it shall be given unto you, pressed down, shaken together and running over ...' (Lk 6:38). The canonists considered charity an act of love (in its original sense) or in the legal sense an act of divine justice.

Furthermore the canonists declared that for a work of charity to be meritorious, it had to be motivated by a right attitude to God and neighbour, and the giver had to purify his heart from sin. There was no room for bribing heaven, and Gratian quoted St Ambrose, 'It is not enough to do good unless the act flows from a good source, that is good will,' and St Augustine, 'If it is given without a loving heart it is altogether insufficient.'[4] To give alms simply to be rid of an importunate beggar, without charity in the heart, was actually sinful. Almsgiving, to avoid vainglory, must uphold justice, order, and right intention; justice meant that the giver's property had to be justly acquired; order meant that the giver had to order his life spiritually; and right intention meant that the giver had to give from motives of true charity, rather than to win praise or to fob off an inconvenience.[5]

The canonists considered two elements in the almsgiver: the renunciation of part of his property and the act of compassion for one in need. The first element applied particularly to those entering the religious life, in which it was proper to renounce all worldly goods, the second element however required 'discretion' when the donor acted in compassion for another's need, and required the donor to give a little at a time in order to help the maximum number.[6]

The mediaeval church was well aware of the distinction between evangelical poverty and idleness. Walter Daniel, for example, biographer of St Ailred of Rievaulx, said of the Cistercians 'They venerate poverty, not the penury of the idle and negligent, but a poverty directed by a necessity of the will and sustained by the thoroughness of faith, and approved by divine love.'[7] St Francis in his devotion to voluntary evangelical poverty declared in his last testament, 'I have worked with my hands and I choose to work, and I firmly wish that all my brothers should work at some honourable trade.'[8]

The framers of the mediaeval poor law distinguished between voluntary and involuntary poverty and focused their efforts on relieving the evils of involuntary poverty, which unlike evangelical poverty, was far from inducing virtue. Thus the canonist Huguccio (d. 1210) divided the poor into those born into poverty, who endured their state for the love of God; those who joined themselves to the poor by giving up all their possessions to follow Christ; and those who were filled with the 'voracity of cupidity.'[9] The medieval canonists did not consider poverty as a vice or fault of character requiring eradication, an attitude very different from that of a later age which viewed poverty as a defect greatly to be abhorred. Johannes Andreae, following St Ambrose, stated, 'Poverty is not among the number of things evil:'[10] in other words, no moral guilt attached to the sufferer.

The canonists well understood that indiscriminate charity destroys its own ends and they were concerned not to encourage idle vagabondage. A gross injustice was therefore done by nineteenth century writers who described mediaeval charity as naive and indiscriminate, and treated the new Poor Law of Elizabeth I, and its subsequent development, as inspired innovation which gave the world a basis for social legislation.[11] Yet Cardinal Ehrle and Professor Tierney have shown that the Church had always taught discretion in almsgiving.[12]

Gratian urged donors not to give everything at once. Johannes Teutonicus required that only plain and simple food should be offered to the poor, not dainties. Hostiensis commented that reckless generosity was not noble, but the act of a fool. The *Glossa Ordinaria* said very specifically: 'The Church ought not to provide for a man who is able to work, ... for strong men sure of their food without work often do neglect justice.'[13] This admonition can be compared to St Paul's teaching. 'If a man does not work then neither shall he eat' (2 Th 3:10). From this can be derived the surest defence against the charge of fostering pauperism, for the canonists plainly condemned wilful idleness.

St John Chrysostom however had upheld the giving of alms to all without restraint, and this led the canonists to debate how far to discriminate. Surely St John Chrysostom's teaching was the ideal and, like much Roman law, could also be tempered to individual needs, a general maxim with an individual application with its own intrinsic restraints.

Rufinus' commentary on the *Decretum* explained that to avoid indiscriminate generosity the donor must consider four things:

> the quality of the one asking—whether he is honest or dishonest; the resources of the one giving—whether they can suffice for all or only for some; the cause of the request, whether a man asks only for food for the love of God ... the amount requested—whether it is excessive or reasonable. If the one who asks is dishonest, and especially if he is able to seek his food by his own labour and neglects to do so, so that he chooses rather to beg or steal, without doubt nothing is to be given to him, but he is to be corrected ... unless perchance he is close to perishing from want, for then, if we have anything we ought to give indifferently to all

such ... But if the one who asks is honest, you ought to give to all of this sort if the available resources suffice ...[14]

Raymund de Pennaforte (1175–1275), who compiled the *Gregorian Decretals*, sums up the problem of applying discretion as follows:

> Either you have enough for all or not. In the first case you ought to give to all indiscriminately ... this is true except, when by being made sure of his food a man would neglect justice, for in that case 'it is more useful to take away bread from the needy etc' except when he is dying of hunger, for then he ought to be fed however much he may neglect justice.[15]

St Ambrose's system was carefully applied: healthy but idle beggars were to be refused, but deserving beggars were to be helped depending on what was available. If there was enough for all, St John Chrysostom's principle of indiscriminate aid was applied except with regard to idle and nefarious persons, who were only to be fed if *in extremis*.

The undeserving were listed as: excommunicated priests who were a burden on their bishops; spendthrifts living in wanton extravagance; and unbeneficed clergy made poor by gambling. Clergy in particular had a habit of wandering about in lay clothes demanding support, and canonists suggested that they be carefully examined and excessive demands refused. Despite their folly or wickedness, however, the undeserving (and this included pagans) should *in extremis* be given charity; in less extreme circumstances they should labour in want, for as the canonists rightly observed, if they were healthy they should earn their bread by their own labour (before industrialization and population density introduced the modern phenomenon of unemployment). Refusal of alms or provender was only prescribed in cases where the mendicant was healthy and charity could encourage idleness or wickedness.[16] Gratian added that, depending on the resources of the benefactor, the undeserving should wait their turn. This was a more enlightened system of charity than its nineteenth century counterpart, for the evidence suggests that it did not deter those in genuine need.

Guido de Baysio (1250–1313) explained that the indiscriminate charity of St John Chrysostom was to be applied to 'day-to-day alms,' to the sums that a man might give away on a daily basis; whereas when a man was considering making a major donation, he should exercise careful discrimination. In other words, the abuse of charity could be tolerated in small measure but not in a case of major assistance. In this the canonists' principle was, 'In case of doubt it is better to do too much than do nothing at all.'[17]

In debating the difference between the 'deserving' and the 'undeserving' poor, Gratian was much guided by St Ambrose, one of the greatest of the fourth century exponents of poor relief. The *Decretum* maintained the teaching of the Fathers, and of St John Chrysostom, St Ambrose and St Augustine in particular, and gives evidence of continuity of practice from the early Church to the Middle Ages.

Notes

[1] An earlier draft of this chapter was published in *Faith* magazine, January 1987.

[2] B. Tierney, *Medieval Poor Law* (Berkeley and Los Angeles, University of California Press, 1959), pp. 7–8.

3   Quoted *ibid.*, p. 15.
4   *Ibid.*, pp. 52–53.
5   *Ibid.*, p. 53.
6   *Ibid.*, pp. 49–50.
7   *The Life of Ailred of Rievaulx by Walter Daniel*, trans. & ed. F.M. Powicke (Oxford, Clarendon Press, 1978), [f65b] p. 11; quoted by B. Tierney, p. 142, n. 9.
8   *Opuscula Sancti Patris Francisci* (Quaracchi, 1904), p. 79; trans. B. Tierney, p. 11.
9   Quoted in B. Tierney, p. 11.
10 Quoted *ibid.*, pp. 12–13.
11 See, for example, W. Ashley, *An Introduction to English Economic History and Theory*, 4th ed. (London, Longmans Green, 1906), vol. II, pp. 165–166.
12 Franz Ehrle, *Beitrage zur Geschichte und Reform* (Freiburg, 1881); B. Tierney, pp. 47–49, 53–62.
13 B. Tierney, p. 58.
14 Quoted *ibid.*, p. 59.
15 Quoted *ibid.*, p. 60.
16 *Ibid.*, pp. 60–61.
17 *Ibid.*, pp. 61–62.

Chapter 9

Poor Relief in Mediaeval England

THE VISION THAT inspired the Church's service to the poor was much more than kindness, it was an obligation of the Church with a universal view of sin and suffering in which Christ's redemptive work must continue by succouring those in need with shared benefits.

'The first social problem,' as Ernst Troeltsch put it, 'with which the Church had to deal was the problem of property. It was an extremely difficult problem, and it was only solved amid much hesitation and uncertainty.'[1] In the early Church the few with property spent themselves in the service of the needy, as St Paul testifies. However as the Church grew so did the number of property owners, and the Fathers stressed that property must be regarded as a gift from God to be used for charitable purposes. Detachment from possessions was taught so that like the Stoics they had 'property although they had it not.' The Church at this period therefore came to receive large possessions from wealthy converts who after the Emperor Constantine acquired many properties.

The transition from a Roman to a mediaeval civilization posed some problems for the Church, for the concept of feudalism was based on the private possession of property, unlike the early Church with its communal ownership. Communal ownership was incompatible with the feudal economy of the Middle

Ages. Property thus came to be tortuously explained on the basis of natural law but was nevertheless linked to the obligation of charity. This gave the canonists considerable difficulty in framing an acceptable doctrine. Notwithstanding, the charitable obligations of property owners as framed by the canonists contributed to a great outpouring of private charity during the Middle Ages, for the Church's property was used for all manner of charitable works. Many a great lord would give land to the Church out of genuine piety or as a popular form of supposed spiritual insurance. This enabled the Church to become one of the greatest landlords, and some cathedrals and abbeys owned sufficient land to place their bishops and abbots on a par with the great lords.

In 1224 the Franciscan Order settled in England and from this Order sprang the radical notion of the poverty of Christ. The canonists thus found themselves debating whether Christ and his apostles held property in common or not. The Franciscan theologians defended the poverty of Christ and condemned the great possessions of some abbots and bishops. Such possessions had come to be accepted, so it would seem, but the Franciscan doctrine of the absolute poverty of Christ persisted until 1323, when Pope John XXII condemned a particular form of this doctrine and so brought an end to the debate.

The argument can be traced back to 1210 when Pope Innocent III gave St Francis permission to live according to the simplicity of the Gospel. St Francis' main concern, as was that of his early followers, was to imitate Christ in personal asceticism and to share the life of the poor; later protagonists hardened their attitude in the face of a more relaxed interpretation considered inconsistent with the original inspiration. Schism inevitably followed and despite papal intervention the Franciscan Order split, some joining the Spirituals or *Fraticelli*, thus discrediting the concept of absolute poverty. St Francis lived out the Gospel ideal but some later extremists made evangelical poverty an end in itself. Today the Franciscans have all the benefits of ownership but claim the Church as the possessor of their property.[2]

In this problem of the ownership of Church property the canonists insisted that bishops and priests had no absolute rights of ownership, but acted as trustees. In which case who then was the owner? St Augustine insisted that, 'The things of which we have charge do not belong to us but to the poor.' St Ambrose made the qualification, 'The Church has gold, not to hoard away, but to share out and help those in need;' St Jerome went further, 'Whatever the clergy have belongs to the poor, and their houses ought to be common to all.'[3] Here there is perhaps a need to distinguish the ideal from the practical doctrine. The possessions of the Church were public property, dominion being vested in the whole Christian community with Christ at its head. The bishops and the clergy were therefore administrators on behalf of Christ for the benefit of those in need—this in broad terms came to be the canonists' explanation of ownership, with the poor, at least in theory, remaining the chief beneficiaries.

The mediaeval system of poor relief retained the bishop as a special dispenser of charity, for although religious houses and private charities served the poor in answer to the Church's teachings, the parishes under their respective bishops provided a network of poor relief throughout England. The *Decretum* still bound bishops to assist the needs of widows and orphans and the poor in general, adding that if a man lacked 'hospitality' he should not receive the episcopal office.[4]

Hospitality in this sense referred to the care of poor wayfarers or pilgrims, which was also binding on all parish clergy. The bishops, as in earlier days, were supposed to divide the total revenue of the diocese into four parts with a portion allotted to the poor. The tithe system followed this allocation, but in practice had largely devolved upon the parish clergy, for few diocesan bishops honoured these principles of poor relief. In fact lay patronage diverted much parish revenue, which instead of supplying poor relief frequently supported an absentee parson. A particular abuse was the appropriation of parishes by monastic foundations which despite having pioneered much poor relief in some cases actually diverted parish revenues that would otherwise have served the poor.

The Fourth Lateran Council of 1215 did much to remedy the abuse of absenteeism and moreover declared that the clergy were to keep hospitality (*tenere hospitalitatem*). Despite the decline in monastic care for the poor by the thirteenth century there are no recorded complaints of neglect from those who presented themselves at the gates of the greater monasteries. The later *Valor Ecclesiasticus,* ordered by Henry VIII for tax purposes, was the most complete investigation of the value of monastic properties and their income in England. It showed that some 3–5% of total income was spent on the poor, but this is an inadequate picture as it takes no account of the daily distribution of food and alms to poor travellers. Moreover the *Valor Eccle-*

siasticus for the most part chronicles particular bequests and entertainment expenses.

During the twelfth and thirteenth centuries the Church's work of charity was greatly assisted by the foundation of religious hospitals. The Order of St John in this became an exemplar for they ran two hospitals in Jerusalem and another outside the walls, not to mention a field hospital staffed by surgeons who accompanied the Christian armies, a burial ground, a primitive ambulance service, an orphanage, a school and a major almonry. Unlike the monasteries and other religious houses the hospitals often spent all their revenue on the people they cared for and still managed to feed the poor travellers who called each day. Such institutions were not adequately accounted for in canon law until quite late, although there was provision for the local bishop to intervene where there was a suspicion of embezzlement.

Pope Clement V's Bull *Quia Contingit* of 1311 directed all bishops to enquire into the running of hospitals in their dioceses and correct any abuses. Subsequently wardens of hospitals had to take a solemn oath to exercise their duties with diligence, with particular regard for administration, and were bound to produce an annual statement of accounts for the local bishop; of particular interest was the papal ruling that the office of warden should not be regarded as an ecclesiastical benefice. This decretal protected the income of the hospital from being diverted to support the career of some ambitious cleric, but allowed for the payment of a reasonable stipend to the warden and his assistants; moreover it also allowed for a layman to exercise the office of warden. In this way the wishes of the founder could be respected and the income wholly devoted to the foundation's intended charitable purpose.

Hospitals, in general therefore did not suffer the abuses which so commonly afflicted the charity of parishes and other religious houses in the work of poor relief.

In the mid-fourteenth century the canonist Lapus de Castellione, in his *De Hospitalitate,* outlined hospital law and emphasised the supervision of the local bishop as part of a public service, an inheritance from the early Church. The law is concerned largely with property, administration and privileges, which has left its mark on modern legislation. Although the law gives little detail on daily problems of hospitaller work, or the kind of ministry conducted from monasteries or hospitals, it is known that the rules governing admission were more compassionate than the workhouse tests of a later period.

Christian charity, rather than secular paternalism, was the intended principle throughout and although lavishness was eschewed this was only to ensure resources could be more widely distributed. Parish poor relief, wrote Cardinal Gasquet, 'was fully accepted and carried out.'[5] This has often been challenged but records of parish visitations for the most part make no mention of neglect, while various episcopal registers show evidence of constant vigilance in this matter.

In fact, when Pope Innocent IV imposed a particularly heavy tax payment on the English clergy, they defended themselves by pointing to their reputation for hospitality:

> Since a custom has heretofore prevailed and been observed in England, that the rectors of parochial churches have always been remarka-

ble for hospitality, and have made a practice of supplying food to their parishioners who were in want, ... if a portion of their benefices be taken away from them, they will be under the necessity of refusing their hospitality, and abandoning their accustomed offices of piety. And if these be withdrawn, they will incur the hatred of those subject to them, and will lose the favour of passers-by and their neighbours ... to the disgrace and loss of the Church universal.[6]

In feudal England land ownership constituted power, and all land was vested in the crown. The great lords were the chief tenants therefore and so on down by the process of subinfeudation. The manor lordships, into which the country was divided, in those days possessed a geographical integrity consisting of the smallest composite unit in the system. The lords of the manor invariably held their land in return for military service (or fee simple). This service was given to the local overlord who in turn held his land from an even greater lord (*mutatis mutandis*) who held direct from the Crown.

The manor land was subdivided into strips of twenty of twenty to thirty acres and these were held by serfs or villeins in return for agricultural service on the lord's desmesne. The serf was a bondsman and was not free to leave the manor as he was 'bound to the soil.' To obtain his freedom a serf could flee to a neighbouring town where after a year and a day he would be declared a 'freeman'. Likewise he could obtain freedom in the unlikely event of him seeking the priesthood. Not infrequently these feudal obligations were commuted to money payment, which did not leave the mediaeval peasant free to wander. Thus with the threat of destitution on the roads most preferred to enjoy the benefits of their smallholding. These self-supporting agricultural communities would suffer great hardship in the event of a bad harvest, particularly the serfs and the villeins.

The social and economic conditions of the later middle ages made poor relief a much more complex problem and canon law failed to keep pace with the changes. The manorial system began to decline, villeins in many cases managed to commute their agricultural service to monetary rents, and lords of the manor not infrequently leased their lands to farmers for a fixed rent, thus leading to the replacement of the old land economy by a money economy.

The Black Death (1348–9), a bubonic plague which came to England by the port of Weymouth and was carried through the country by disease-laden rats, caused immense hardship. The death rate was so high that by 1400 England's population was reduced by nearly half. The poorer people who survived in the villages and on the land were the worst affected and so the soil was left untilled and the livestock untended. This led to a rise in wages and villeins abandoning their native land-holding to offer their services to the highest bidder. Some poor labourers did not even look for work but roamed in bands begging and robbing by turns. The state reacted with alarm and passed the Statute of Labourers of 1349, which bound all such men to stay and work for their local landlord:

> Every man or woman of whatsoever condition, free or bond, able in body and within age of three score years, and not having of his own whereof he may live, nor land of his own about the tillage of which he may occupy himself, and

not serving any other shall be bound to serve the employer who shall require him to do so, and shall take only the wages which were accustomed to be taken in the neighbourhood where he is bound to serve.[7]

Little was achieved by this legislation and within two years the old law, which bound each man to his own village, was reapplied. To this were added harsher penalties, such as branding on the forehead for any who tried to flee. This treatment incensed the peasantry and a priest of Kent, one John Ball, incited the mob with his trenchant sermon:

> Ah, all ye good people, matters goeth not well in England, nor shall do until everything be common and there be no villeins nor gentlemen. We be all come from one father and mother, Adam and Eve. The lords are clothed in velvet and stuffs trimmed with fur, but we in poor cloth. They have their wines, spices and good bread; and we have bread made from chaff and only water to drink.[8]

Subsequently a poll-tax of one shilling was levied upon everyone, which led to one of the earliest risings of the poor in England, the Peasants' Revolt. These rebels of 1381 were ruthlessly put down, but in the aftermath of the Black Death such was the shortage of labour that many a villein redressed his financial grievances by offering his services to a land lord prepared to pay higher wages.

In the general chaos the highways were filled with vagabonds seeking the fleeting opportunities of the time. The problem of vagrancy was aggravated by the return of soldiers from the Hundred Years War; moreover these with their fighting experience probably induced fear in fellow-travellers and local residents. With the increase in robbery and violence there was a noticeable decline in sympathy for the homeless. The change in the agrarian economy also saw the enclosure of pasture, which had previously been common land, thus forcing the poor off the land that had previously supported them.

The higher wages generally improved the lot of the poor. Moreover by the fifteenth century serfdom was almost non-existent, except for the few who fell behind the rising tide of affluence with a life of abject misery. Sudden changes in the economy did bring a general improvement but often also eradicated old safeguards against total destitution. Thus the break-up of the manorial system undermined the surviving security of the elderly and impotent. The later middle ages therefore had to deal with the conflicting moral demands of succouring the poor on the one hand and on the other suppressing the scourge of vagabondage, by which homelessness became an ever increasing feature of daily life.

Apart from these setbacks fourteenth century England could boast of up to 800 hospitals, which was more *per capita* than in many parts of the world today; moreover it could be claimed that there was one bed for every 600 citizens.

Notes

[1] Ernest Troeltsch, *The Social Teaching of the Christian Churches*, trans. O. Wyon (London, George Allen & Unwin Ltd, 1931), vol. 1, p. 115.

[2] For a detailed account of the controversy, see M. D. Lambert, *Franciscan Poverty; the Doctrine of the Absolute Poverty of Christ and the Apostles in the Franciscan Order 1210–1323*, rev. and

expanded ed. (New York, St Bonaventure University, 1998).
3   Quoted by B. Tierney, p. 40.
4   *Ibid.*, p. 68.
5   F. A. Gasquet, *Parish Life in Mediaeval England*, 6th ed. (London, Methuen & Co, 1929), p. 84.
6   Matthew Paris, sub anno 1246, from *Matthew Paris's English History, from 1235–73*, trans. J. A. Giles, 3 vols. (London, Henry G. Bohn, 1852–4), vol. 2, p. 193. For a survey of comparable developments on the continent from the twelfth to the mid-fourteenth century, see M. Mollat, *The Poor in the Middle Ages: An Essay in Social History*, trans. from the French by A. Goldhammer (New Haven and London, Yale University Press, 1986), pp. 115–190.
7   Quoted in G. Kent, *Poverty* (London, Batsford, 1968), p. 18.
8   Quoted *ibid.*, p. 19.

CHAPTER 10

THE DISSOLUTION AND ITS SOCIAL CONSEQUENCES IN ENGLAND

DESPITE PAPAL LEGISLATION the fifteenth century saw an increase in pluralism and absenteeism, with the sees of Worcester and Salisbury being held *in commendam* by absentee Italian prelates at the Crown's behest. Although bishops had obtained control over most of the hospitals many of the greater foundations obtained their independence. The consequence of this was that revenues, without proper scrutiny, were diverted to administrators. Standards declined and a spirit of compromise came to affect the strict interpretation of canon law. Moreover with a shortage of vocations less qualified men moved into positions of responsibility. Bishops often seemed tainted with careerism and bureaucracy sapped the Church's vitality and vitiated its evangelical mission. In this general decline hospitality often failed and the poor were inevitably neglected. The mediaeval poor law as a consequence failed to develop to meet the changing social and economic conditions, and although the tradition of hospitality continued its effectiveness diminished, and there is some justification for the disparagement of the effectiveness of the Church's social ministry at this time.

There were nevertheless only isolated instances of laxity and embezzlement, and by and large substantial amounts of money, food, and clothing were regularly distributed to the needy. On the very eve of the dissolution some monasteries devoted a considerable part of their income to the poor. At the Cistercian house of Merevale in Warwickshire three thousand herrings with bread and beer were distributed each Maundy Thursday with five shillings for each poor man; added to this was the weekly dole of bread and beer. Moreover fifty pounds was allocated to the monastery's wayfarers' hospice,[1] which indicates that where resources were well husbanded and the economy had been maintained, despite the changes in society, religious houses could still make a major contribution to hospitality.

The hospitals, like some of the other religious houses, had by the eve of the Reformation lost some of their original zeal and efficiency. A number had become run down or had been isolated by movements of population; what is more, with the end of the plague and the decline in leprosy, some had ceased to serve their original purpose. Some had become sinecures, providing a steady income for absentee wardens; others had been re-founded, or amalgamated, or even closed down altogether. Meanwhile large religious hospitals such as at St Leonard's, York, Newark, and the Savoy Hospital in London continued to flourish.[2] The spectre of dissolution might have sapped the energy of some establishments but new initiatives continued, notably in the cases of almshouses and of provision for orphans and the insane.

In this there is ample evidence of adaptation to changing needs, and of advances which were lost at the dissolution. The Savoy Hospital pioneered much new work and men and women were not lacking to serve the poor and the sick as a religious vocation. No doubt the hospitals and hospitaller communities would have experienced a renewal in England following the upsurge of religious vitality in the new foundations of Italy and France, but the scourge of the Reformation proved insuperable.[3]

Tragically, the Catholic establishment had already pioneered the dissolution of English religious houses in the interests of efficiency, little knowing the use that would be made of the precedents that they had set. Bishop St John Fisher with Lady Margaret Beaufort had used the monies of decayed houses to found Christ's and St John's colleges at Cambridge; while Cardinal Wolsey dissolved twenty-nine religious houses for his new foundations of Ipswich School and Cardinal College (re-named Christ Church after his death). The houses Wolsey dissolved, such as Bayham Abbey, founded c. 1208 on the borders of Kent and Sussex by Robert de Turnham for the White Canons of Premontre, were in fact far from decayed. The local population had risen in protest but papal sanction had already been granted.

Many failing hospitals had also been suppressed and their properties transferred to other foundations. For example the leper hospitals at Windsor and Huntingdon were annexed to Cambridge colleges in 1462; the hospitals at Romney, Aynho, and Brackley, were appropriated to Magdalen College, Oxford, between 1481 and 1485; and St John's Hospital, Reading, and St Bartholomew's, Bristol, were converted into schools by 1532.[4]

The monastic houses may sometimes have been poor at channelling their wealth, which was largely derived from benefactions, towards the needy, and in some of the houses there may also have been a certain endemic laxity (no more than there is today, perhaps less). The report on the smaller houses, which was contrived by the King's creature Thomas Cromwell and his fawning cronies and declared the houses to be in an evil condition, was nevertheless hasty and heavily biased and there was certainly no justification for wholesale dissolution. The drastic action which was taken can perhaps only be explained by Henry VIII's desire to achieve supremacy over the Church in England and to replenish the royal coffers.

The majority of hospitals functioned well and the *Valor Ecclesiasticus* records that in most cases monies were spent on worthy charitable causes. Had justice been done any minor examples of mismanagement could have been remedied and the establishments could have become doubly beneficent in the face of the demise of monastic charity.

Royal supremacy over the Church in England had been achieved by 1534, and the First Act of Suppression 1536 suppressed some two hundred houses with an annual value of less than £200, prompting the Pilgrimage of Grace in October 1536, a popular rising originating in the counties of Yorkshire and Lincolnshire. Deception, intrigue and butchery on the part of the monarch finally dispersed the Pilgrimage's adherents; meanwhile Parliament passed the Second Act of Suppression 1539 and royal agents pressed on with the dissolution of the greater houses, with the result that by 1540 the last religious house had been dissolved.

The monasteries had owned one-fifteenth of all the land and the Cistercians, in particular, had been skilful agricultural pioneers. The Dissolution cut off the main supply of food, alms, and shelter for the poor and indigent and enormous suffering ensued. The sick and poor wayfarer could no longer turn to religious hospitals for care and shelter. The new tenants of the old monastic lands dismissed labourers and demolished cottages in order to graze sheep, a heartless practice of enclosure which made many poor people completely destitute. These dispossessed poor would drift from town to town looking for work, as Philip Stubbs recorded in 1583: 'They lie in the streets in the dirt as commonly seen ... and are permitted to die like dogs or beasts without any mercy or compassion showed them at all.'[5]

These changes saw a large increase in the number of 'sturdy vagabonds' roaming the country. Beggars had been a common sight in the towns but never before had such numbers of healthy vagrants swelled the highways, sleeping in barns and hedgerows, begging their food and not infrequently menacing any local citizens who failed to give them succour. A few contemporary lines sum up the popular impression:

> Hark, hark the dogs do bark,
> The beggars are coming to town.
> Some in rags and some in tags
> And some in silken gowns.

The Chantries Act 1545 for the dissolution of hospitals, guilds and chantries, was followed by the Chantries Act 1547 for the expropriation of guilds, chantries and any surviving colleges of secular clergy. The demise of the guilds further exacerbated the lot of the poor, for a number of guilds had helped to support the humble craftsmen and to finance charitable institutions. There is plenty of evidence to show the unpopularity of the Dissolution particularly in relation to the administration of poor relief. Lord Audley in 1538 wrote pleading for the Benedictine house of Colchester since it gave daily relief to 'many poure people' and gave needed hospitality to the surrounding communities,[6] while many other lay people wrote asking for particular houses to be spared.[7]

The hospitals were largely destroyed in the 1530s. York lost thirteen hospitals including St Leonard's where forty-five poor people had been cared for. The Chantries Acts of 1545 and 1547 also caused the closure of hospitals, because such charitable foundations were often attached to chantries. Some hospitals re-opened in a Protestant form some years later, as in Abingdon, Leicester and Lambourne. In London it took over nine years to recover some of the dissolved hospitals. Sir Richard Gresham, Lord Mayor of London, pleaded with King Henry VIII to 'let the Mayor and Corporation have rule of St Mary's Spital, St Bartholomew, St Thomas and Towerhill, which were founded in London for the aid of poor wretched people.'[8] St Bartholomew's, still on its original site, St Thomas's, now on the Thames Embankment, and St Mary of Bethlehem (Bedlam), now in Beckenham, Kent, were re-opened after poor sick wayfarers from the shires blocked the city's roads, but this was only after special pleading with the king.

The Western Rebellion in 1549 was much more than a protest against the Prayer Book of Edward VI. The men of Cornwall could not understand the English of this imposed book and wanted the restoration of Catholic religion together with the revival of religious houses. The rebellion was put down with extreme brutality and priests in their vestments were hanged from their steeples across the Cornish peninsula. In general it was the land owners who benefited from the chaos of unregulated land grabbing.

Post-reformation historians have largely failed to appreciate the hardships caused by these tragic times but G. Baskerville does at least observe:

> The question of how far hospitality and almsgiving suffered by the suppression is a very difficult question and can never be satisfactorily answered ... under the Act of Suppression of 1536 the grantees of monastic lands were bound to keep an honest continual house and household in the same site and precinct. Thus it was intended that inn keeping should still be a condition of land holding. Whether it was fulfilled may be doubted. But in any case ... individual hospitality on the grand scale was falling into disuse. When Henry VIII went to Dunstable in the summer of 1537 he preferred to put up at the White Horse Inn rather than at the priory ... In the north, the result of the suppression must have been far more felt and in particular by the poorer sort of travellers. Just as the grantees of monastic lands were expected to keep up hospitality, so, apparently, were they expected to go on with the old system of doles.[9]

This was doubtless a slightly forlorn hope in the wake of many grasping lawyers who became landed over night through the acquisition of abbey spoil.

Contemporary Protestant reformers witnessed to the misery of the poor. Bishop Hugh Latimer, in one of his sermons, asked:

> ... is there not reigning in London, as much pride, as much covetousness, as much cruelty, as much oppression and as much superstition as was in Nebo? Yes, I think, and much more too

... But London was never so ill as it is now. In times past men were full of pity and compassion, but now there is no pity; for in London their brother shall die in the streets for cold, he shall lie sick at the door between stock and stock, I cannot tell what to call it, and perish there for hunger: was there ever more unmercifulness in Nebo? I think not. In times past, when any rich man died in London, they were wont to help the poor scholars of the Universities with Exhibition. When any man died, they would bequeath great sums of money toward the relief of the poor ... but now charity is waxen cold, none helpeth the scholar, nor yet the poor.

John Bradford, another English reformer, wrote:

All men may see that immorality in its foulest forms, pride, dishonesty, unmercifulness, scoffing at religion and virtue, and a desire to oppress and crush down the poor, far surpassed at this time anything that before occurred in the realm.[10]

In a letter to Archbishop Cranmer the same author said:

A heavy curse seems to have fallen on the people; I know not what to think. Desolation overshadows this land of ours, that was ever so prosperous and contented.

Camden, the Protestant annalist, describing King Edward VI's reign, wrote,

But sacrilegious avarice ravenously invaded Church livings, colleges, chantries, hospitals and places dedicated to the poor, as superstitious. Ambition and emulation among the nobility, presumption and disobedience among the common people, were so insolent that England seemed in a kind of frenzy.¹¹

Thus even Protestant reformers described a sorry state: where, in earlier times, great institutions had disbursed relief to the poor, a forlorn state of desolation reigned to obliterate the memory of things past.

Notes

1. J. J. Scarisbrick, *The Reformation and the English People* (Oxford, Basil Blackwell, 1984) pp. 51–52.
2. *Ibid.*, p. 53.
3. For a survey of comparable developments on the continent from the mid-fourteenth to the early sixteenth century, see Mollat, M., *The Poor in the Middle Ages: An Essay in Social History*, trans. from the French by A. Goldhammer (New Haven and London, Yale University Press, 1986), pp. 191–293.
4. R. M. Clay, *The Mediaeval Hospitals of England* (Frank Cass & Co. Ltd, London, 1966), p. 226.
5. G. Kent, p. 21.
6. J. J. Scarisbrick, p. 71.
7. *Ibid.*, p. 73.
8. Quoted in G. Baskerville, *English Monks and the Suppression of the Monasteries* (London, Jonathan Cape, 1965) p. 279.
9. *Ibid.*, pp. 278–279. For a modern account of contemporary changes in the theory and practice of hospitality, see F. Heal, *Hospitality in Early Modern England* (Oxford, Clarendon Press, 1990).
10. For this and the following quotation, see *Historical Portraits of the Tudor Dynasty and the Reformation Period*, by S. H. Burke (London, John Hodges, 1880), vol. II, p. 297. Burke's source for these quotations is uncertain: neither can be found in the two-volume Parker Society edition of Bradford's works (ed. A. Townsend, Cambridge, 1848–53).
11. W. Camden, *The Life and Reign of that Excellent Princess Queen Elizabeth* (London, 1738), p. 34.

CHAPTER 11

POST-REFORMATION CRISIS IN ENGLAND

PARLIAMENT HAD PUT Henry VIII in possession of the monasteries and chantries fondly believing that he intended to improve the hospitals, to 'bringe them into a more decent and convenient order,'[1] and the new owners of the lands and properties of the former religious houses were initially expected to continue to provide the same hospitality for the poor as the previous occupants had. In the draft of the Suppression Bill 1539 it had been proposed that the greater monasteries that survived should build bede houses to provide for ten poor men who had reached sixty years of age. Such charitable benefit could have relieved part of the suffering but invariably such redemptive aspirations were overlooked. More often than not the plundering of religious foundations robbed the poor of vital support. Even if Henry VIII expressed a desire to relieve the plight of the poor, his actions would seem to contradict any genuine intention.

Henry Brinklow, a citizen of London, bemoaning the increased deprivation of the poor in 1545, published *The Lamentacyon of a Christian against the Cytye of London*. In this he wrote:

> London, beying one of the flowers of the worlde, as touchinge wordlye riches, hath so manye, yea innumerable of poore people forced to go from dore to dore, and to syt openly in the streets a beggynge, and many ... lye in their howses in

most greuous paynes, and dye for lacke of ayde of the riche. I thinke in my judgement, under heaven is not so lytle prouision made for the pore as in London, of so riche a Cytie.[2]

Then in 1546 Brinklow published *A Supplication of the Poore Commons*. This describes the plight of the sick and poor in greater penury than ever. Before the Dissolution they 'had hospitals, and almshouses to be lodged in, but nowe they lye in the streets.' Brinklow continued to protest that the portion given to poor impotent folk, the lame, blind, lazar and sore members of Christ, who once had been lodged in hospitals and almshouses, was now given by the King and his nobles to grasping opportunists.[3]

Many hospitals and their revenues found their way into the hands of royal favourites. Some were dissolved with the smaller priories in 1536, some were dissolved with the great monastic houses in 1539, and some went with the chantries, chapels, and guild properties, in 1545. They were swept away without discrimination and without any consistent planning. The Savoy Hospital in London was dissolved just after building was complete and the leper hospital of St James was dissolved in 1532 as the King was impatient to build himself a new palace on the site.

The London hospitals which did re-open were revived not so much by the initiative of the King but rather by the benevolence and generosity of the Mayor and the citizens of London. Thus at least in the City of London, where the sick and poor lay in the streets and citizens were molested for alms and traversed the streets in danger of infection, some small remedy was introduced. To those which did re-open were added Christ's Hospital for orphans and Bridewell for vagabonds. Moreover a number of hospitals such as St Mary's, Chichester; St Nicholas's, Salisbury; St Giles, Norwich; St Cross, Winchester; and St John's, Canterbury, became almshouses.

No state relief had been necessary before the Reformation as the poor law was enshrined in the canons of the Church. This was largely effective up to the thirteenth century, when the feudal system with all its inadequacies did create a mutual dependence, when the serf, villein, and yeoman came under the protection of the local lord, who in turn served a greater lord, all coming under the protection of the King. The religious houses and hospitals supplied the greater part of poor relief in terms of food and shelter and these were invariably founded by great lords or the King. Parish relief was largely limited to doles of food or money. The serfs and villeins worked on the land confined to their place of birth and were obliged to work for fixed wages as determined by local justices, who as landowners provided the employment. Changes in the social and economic conditions did however disrupt the security of these conditions, for instance the Black Death virtually ended this land economy. Villeins for instance took advantage of the decimation of labourers by the plague to leave their villages and sell their services to the highest bidder. The conditions were exacerbated by those who sought a roaming life, begging and stealing as they went. The Statute of Cambridge 1388 prohibited begging and wayfaring and Bridewell Hospital was founded for the correction of idle vagabonds.[4]

In this changed economy landlords would lease their land to farmers for a fixed income, thus laying the foundations of modern capitalism. This dislocation of an agrarian economy continued and reached an apogee at the dissolution of the religious houses. Monasteries had been great employers of labour and their passing not only increased the employment problem but also caused much arable land to be converted into pasture, requiring fewer labourers and forcing more out of work and into destitution.

As the effects of the dissolution began to bite, greater hardship followed with draconian legislation that numerous justices did not always have the heart to enforce. The Punishment of Sturdy Vagabonds and Beggars Act 1536 declared that beggars had increased as a result of idleness, and stipulated that the justices should give a licence to impotent beggars by which they could live on alms within a prescribed area. Thus, if a beggar moved outside his limits, or if an impotent person begged without a licence, he would be whipped or set in the stocks. Any healthy person caught begging would also be whipped through the town and bound on oath to return to his place of birth. Improvident undergraduates at Oxford and Cambridge were similarly dealt with. The Act of 1536 also stipulated a fine for any who gave alms to, or harboured, healthy beggars. A further Act in the same reign made the fine ten times the value of the alms given. Yet another Act in the reign of Edward VI complained of the foolishness of those who support healthy beggars and failed to uphold the law.

Post-Reformation England was no longer under the influence of the Catholic Church and displayed a very different attitude towards poverty. The new legislation was to prove cruel and ineffective.

Notes

1. Quoted in R. M. Clay, *The Mediaeval Hospitals of England* (London, Frank Cass & Co. Ltd, 1966), p. 230.
2. H. Brinklow, in *Henry Brinklow's Complaynt of Roderyck Mors sometyme a gray fryre unto the parliament howse of England ...(about A.D. 1542) and The Lamentacyon of a Christian agaynst the Cytye of London*, ed. J. M. Cowper (London, Early English Text Society, extra ser., 22, 1874), quoted *ibid.*, p. 14.
3. H. Brinklow, *A Supplicacyon for the beggers, with A supplycacion to our moste soveraigne lord Kynge Henry the Eyght, A supplication of the poore commons, ...* ed. J. M. Cowper (London, Early English Text Society, extra ser., 18, 1871), quoted *ibid.*, p. 231.
4. This and the following paragraphs are taken, with minor alterations, from the author's *The Church's Response to the Homeless* (Great Wakering, McCrimmon, 1985), p. 11.

CHAPTER 12

THE ORDER OF ST JOHN

WHEN CHARLES V gave the knights the island of Malta, there was already a hospital on the island but the Order set about building their own at the port of Birgu. Once again the Order's vocation was modified as Malta was not on any of the Christian pilgrimage routes, obviating the need to care for poor wayfarers. The ideal had been found in the Jerusalem foundation, open to sick and poor alike, of any race or religion, but especially to poor travellers. The hospital at Rhodes may have been more exclusive because there is no record of admitting say Moslems and Jews, but the hospital at Malta would seem to have been a genuine forerunner of the modern infirmary. Thus the Order became more associated with a medical ministry than with a ministry of pure hospitality. There had always been a medical element, but this now continued on a wider scale in the infirmaries of the Order, above all in subsidising the medical care of the poor.

The Order built a new infirmary at Valetta in 1575, modelled on the plan of the old hospital at Rhodes but more practical with a large central courtyard, the main ward being on the first floor to which all the others were added, and with a much larger chapel. In this the Order was determined to build what was the best for its time. Again each patient had a single bed and a cubicle curtained off for privacy. Although this new foundation was more concerned with nursing the sick, the Order also cared for the poor and elderly and the insane, and continued its care of orphans and abandoned infants. The Grand Master and the main community would always be sited next to the hospital.

The chief administrator was the Grand Hospitaller and hospital regulations for the seventeenth century required three physicians and a surgeon to stay every night, and above this five physicians and five surgeons were employed each month who would stay on for three days after the relief team had taken over. There was also an obligatory consultation each week for all physicians.

On Maundy Thursday and on every Sunday from Easter to the Ascension the entire Hospitaller community would pay a ceremonial visit.[1] On entering the Hospital the Grand Master and the great officers would lay aside their rank and enter as simple brothers to assist where they could. Many a knight would voluntarily nurse the sick but the community's greatest involvement was waiting on the sick at meal times. Each patient would have a table spread with a cloth whereon was placed a jug of water and a salt cellar. The food was brought to the centre of the ward and each patient's name would be read out and the diet they had been allocated, then a knight would bear the meal to every patient. Broth in silver bowels was a staple diet as was chicken, and wine would be served in silver goblets.[2]

The Order had a continuous supply of novices who were bound to serve in the wards during their noviciate, with each Langue or national association being assigned a particular day of the week for service in the wards. The novices lodged in the *auberge* or inn of their respective Langue or national association and they were instructed on the rule, statutes, constitution and customs of the Order by their Novice Master and an assortment of knights and chaplains. The novices would follow the Office of the Blessed Virgin Mary in the conventual church where they would attend daily Mass.

Those who wished to accept the vocation of a Hospitaller were addressed as follows:

> Good friend, you desire the company of the House and you are right in this, for many gentlemen earnestly request the reception of their children or their friends and are most joyful when they can place themselves in this Order. And if you are willing to be in so excellent and so honourable a company and so holy an Order as that of the Hospital, you are right in this. But if it is because you see us well clothed, riding on great chargers and having everything for our comfort, then you are misled, for when you would desire to eat, it will be necessary to fast, and when you would wish to fast, you will have to eat. And when you would desire to sleep, it will be necessary to keep watch, and when you would wish to stand on watch, you will have to sleep. And you will be sent here and there, into places which will not please you, and you will have to go there. It will be necessary for you therefore to abandon all your desires to fulfil those of another and to endure other hardships in the Order, more than I can describe to you. Are you willing to suffer all these things?

If the novice accepted these terms he would lay his hand on a missal and make a solemn undertaking as follows:

> I vow to God, to the Blessed Mary ever Virgin, Mother of God, and to St John the Baptist, to render henceforth and for ever, by the grace of God, a true obedience to the superior whom it shall please Him to give me and whom our Religion shall choose, to live without property and to guard my chastity.

The officer of the Order receiving the novice would then say (indicating the cross of the Order),

> Do you believe that this is the Holy Cross upon which Jesus Christ was nailed and died for the redemption of our sins? This is the sign of our Order, which we command you to wear always on your garments.

The novice would then kiss the cross and receive the habit, fastened by a cord around his neck: then he would be addressed as follows:

> Receive the yoke of the Lord, for it is sweet and light, under which you will find rest for your soul. We promise you no delicacies, but only bread and water, and a modest habit of no price.

Upon his reception the new knight would sit on the floor and be served with bread, water and salt.[3]

The Sacred Infirmary, which was more functional than the one at Rhodes and was the equal of the greatest hospitals in Christendom, now established standards of nursing that exceeded all similar foundations in their lavishness and standards of hygiene. The sick were fed on silver dishes, valued for their antiseptic qualities, and lay on clean linen with a tent-like protection for their privacy. Apart from isolation wards there were *lazarettos* for ships needing quarantine conditions. In 1595 the Jesuits established a medical school to which a School of Anatomy was added in the following century,[4] and in the 1660s the great ward of the Hospital was enlarged by five hundred feet, and to this foundation was also added a hospital for women.

Strenuous efforts continued to be made through the eighteenth century to ensure that medical treatment at the Hospital was of the highest order and incorporated the benefits of the latest medical research. For instance there was pioneering surgery for cataracts and Michelangelo Grima, who as chief surgeon introduced the practice of suturing wounds, was one of the most celebrated surgeons of his day.[5]

The seventeenth and eighteenth centuries saw several exemplary members of the Order. Gaspard de Simiane la Coste, who joined the Langue of Provence in 1622, at first dedicated himself to reconciling the Huguenots of his native land and then went to serve in hospitals and prisons and set up a mission to the convicts working the galleys of Marseilles. He established a hospital at Marseilles for sick galley slaves where he carried out his ministry with such unselfishness that he contracted the plague and died in 1649.[6]

Other Hospitallers included six knights who had previously captained the Order's galleys. In the 1690s they lived in community at Valetta under Gabriel du Bois de la Ferte where they led dedicated lives devoted to prayer and the nursing of the sick.

Another knight, Jean-Baptiste de Freslon de la Freslonnniere, was so punctilious with his Hospital duties that in reconciling a dying man he caught a fever and died in 1786. When the city of Messina was destroyed by an earthquake in 1783, his nephew Alexandre de Freslon de la Freslonniere brought galleys full of physicians and medicine and set up a field hospital and food kitchens for the famished citizens.[7]

Although the Order was not originally an order of chivalry in the strict sense it pioneered a 'Gospel chivalry' that provided a spiritual redemption for the class-ridden military code with all its bombast and condescension. Each night in the great Infirmary the knights would recite the following prayer:

> My Lords the Sick, pray God to send peace from heaven to earth. My Lords the Sick, Pray to God to multiply the fruits of the earth so Holy Church will be preserved and people sustained. My Lords the Sick, pray for the Apostle at Rome ... and for all priests, for all kings, for all crusaders, especially for all pilgrims and for all Christians at sea that God bring them to safe harbour, for all prisoners, for all prisoners of the infidel, for souls of their own fathers and mothers and for all who have been good to them, and lastly for the Order and that God may give them a restful night.

In the end it was this spiritualized Gospel chivalry that enabled the Order to survive in a non-combatant role.

The Protestant Reformation had seen many of the Order's assets seized and in 1789 the Order was abolished in France. In 1792 Napoleon captured Malta, having asked for a safe harbour for his fleet, and he then turned against his hosts. Grand Master Ferdinand von Hompesch zu Bolheim capitulated, declaring that the Order's charter forbade any conflict with fellow Christians. He resigned his office and retired to a life of obscurity marking the end of the crusading era. The Order was subsequently dispersed save for a large company of knights who were given shelter by the Russian Czar, Paul I, in St Petersburg, and who subsequently elected him Grand Master. This did not accord with Catholic canon law and Czar Paul was *de facto* rather than *de jure* head of the Order. The Order, with the loss of many of its European priories, then entered a kind of twilight, governed by Lieutenants.

Notes

1. H. J. A. Sire, *The Knights of Malta* (New Haven & London, Yale University Press, 1994), p. 217.
2. *Ibid.*
3. *Ibid.*, pp. 212–213.
4. *Ibid.*, p. 217.
5. *Ibid.*, pp. 217–218.
6. *Ibid.*, p. 219.
7. *Ibid.*, p. 220.

CHAPTER 13

THE NEW POOR LAW IN ENGLAND[1]

AN ACT OF 1551 decreed that every parish should have two or more collectors of alms and should list those in need; each person was expected to contribute according to his capacity. The Elizabethan Poor Laws of 1572, 1597 and 1601 distinguished three types of pauper: those who were too young, too old or too sick to work; those who had lost their jobs through no fault of their own; and those who chose vagrancy as a way of life. The sick and infirm were placed in 'poor-houses'; each parish had to maintain its own poor and a levy was made on the parish (i) 'for burgesses, setting to work the children of all such as whose parents shall not be thought able to keep and maintain them', (ii) 'for setting to work all such persons, married and unmarried, having no means to maintain them, and who use no ordinary and daily trade of life to get their living by', (iii) 'for providing a convenient stock of flax, hemp, wool, thread, iron, and other ware and stuff, to set the poor on work' and (iv) 'for the necessary relief of the lame, impotent, old, blind, and such others among them being poor, and not able to work'. These several objects were supervised by the churchwardens and overseers of the poor from each parish. The justices were empowered 'to commit to the house of correction, or the common gaol, such poor persons as shall not employ themselves to work, being appointed thereunto by the overseers.'[2]

The Poor Law proved, in part, an effective remedy, but could not equal the charity of the religious houses whose disappearance had been the cause of so much suffering and destitution. The Poor Relief Act 1662 (otherwise known as the Settlement and Removal Act) stipulated that, if the overseers complained, the justices might order a person, within forty days of moving to a new parish, back to his original domicile unless security could be given to the new parish against his being a liability. The Poor Law Act 1691 ordered each parish to keep a register of paupers and of the amount of relief given. No name could be added except when the parish officers met every Easter. Once a year was found to be too infrequent and so at the behest of a local justice relief might be given during other times of the year. It was later found that many of the Overseers of the Poor, who administered relief, had become somewhat lax; thus the amount of relief given was to be examined every Easter by the parish officers.

In 1697 a private Act of Parliament permitted the city of Bristol to erect the first workhouse. This provided an incentive to other parishes to follow suit, and so another Act was passed which allowed every parish to provide such dwellings on condition that any poor who refused to enter should *ipso facto* be refused all other relief. This was a far cry from the generosity of the religious houses with their voluntary initiative: now a state charity supported by a tax on ratepayers provided a penny-pinching relief. The ratepayers, anxious to save their pockets, applied the legislation with rigour. The Workhouse Test Act 1723 (also known as Knatchbull's Act) encouraged parishes to put their unemployed to work to mitigate the drain on public charity. The Relief of the Poor Act 1782 (also known as Gilbert's Act) stipulated that none but the old and infirm were to be sent to workhouses: the fit were to have allowances made to them for labouring on the land near their homes. The Removal Act 1795 repealed the Poor Relief Act 1662, under which people were removed to their birthplace so as not to be an expense on the rates, sometimes not even being allowed to die in peace. Under the new Act, persons could not be removed until they had actually come on to the rates, and then only if a justice considered them fit to travel. In that year a party of Berkshire magistrates met at the Pelican Inn at Speenhamland to discuss the salaries of farm workers. They decided that insufficient monies should be supplemented from the rates. In 1796 another Act was passed, granting general out-door relief. The ensuing expense bankrupted villages, ruined landowners, and made the paupers more miserable than ever. A royal commission was appointed to look into the working of the Poor Laws in 1832 and it was found that the Elizabethan Poor Law of 1601 had been seriously mismanaged. There was great disapprobation of healthy paupers, the Protestant work ethic had replaced the indulgent compassion of the religious houses, and swift remedies were introduced.[3]

The Poor Law Amendment Act 1834 provided relief for destitute wayfarers in the 'casual wards' of workhouses. One Poor Law commissioner is quoted as saying: 'our object ... is to establish therein a discipline so severe and repulsive as to make them a terror to the poor and prevent them from entering.'[4] As early as 1866, government vagrancy committees urged reform. They particularly recommended that the casual wards be brought up to a common standard rather than being left to the whims of local authorities. The whole matter, however, was shelved at the outbreak of the First

World War, which for a space cleared the roads of vagrants. The Casual Poor (Relief) Order 1925 attempted some reform in the general standards of the wards. Warm baths were to be provided, and clothes were to be disinfected. Proper sleeping accommodation and better food was to be provided, including a midday meal, but some authorities still insisted that stone breaking and oakum picking should continue.

1926 saw the General Strike, but worse was to follow. By 1929 the international trade depression had affected industry after industry in Britain. Coal mining, shipbuilding, and textile production all came to a halt, and the number of unemployed grew to nearly 3,000,000. By 1929 the number of men regularly out on the road had reached between 50,000 and 60,000. Many of these were too old, infirm, or mentally deficient to find work, but a large proportion were young and vigorous. These were not habitual tramps, but involuntarily unemployed workmen who were genuinely seeking work. In theory the law required them to have somewhere to sleep, and the police moved on those who were forced to sleep rough. If they had a little money they could go to a common lodging house, but the attempt to retain a modicum of decency was frustrated by the fact that these establishments were often dirty and verminous.

The only alternative was the casual ward or reception centre to which they were entitled to go if they had no money. There were about three or four hundred of these casual wards in England at this time; the average distance between them was about fifteen miles, just far enough for a man to be able to walk from one to another in day. Those who could afford it also made use of Salvation Army and Church Army hostels. The casual wards were quite unsuitable for the homeless men and between the wars had a degenerating effect, especially on the younger recently unemployed men from Wales or Tyneside. They had to tramp day after day from one ward to the next, gradually losing self respect and with money gone. By the time winter had set in, petty crime would gain the comparative comfort of a prison cell.

In 1948 the 'casual wards' were renamed reception centres and became the responsibility of the National Assistance Board. Between 1948 and 1979 these centres (run by the Department of Health and Social Security) were reduced from 134 to 23. The Housing (Homeless Persons) Act 1977 has obliged all councils to secure housing for particularly vulnerable homeless single people such as the elderly, the pregnant, or the mentally or physically handicapped. Despite the right of access to housing granted to some single homeless people by this Act, reception centres make no attempt at all to secure the advantage of this significant change in housing policy for those who are admitted. Most of these centres have very low occupancy rates, indicating that even desperate homeless people will shun an archaic system that does not assist them so much as compound their difficulties. By failing to secure permanent housing for homeless people, centres negate the statutory purpose given to them by Parliament in 1948.

There were up to 100,000 single men and women in the 1980s who had been effectively homeless in this country, and many of the centres had remained half empty because unsympathetic conditions drove them away. Many such centres provided accommodation for three nights only, then people were forced to move on; and so this often exacerbated the problem by its very temporary nature. The situation could only worsen with increasing numbers of people unemployed and government cut-backs on public spending. What was needed was extra voluntary support and a revival of the Catholic social ethic to encourage once again a vocation in the service of the homeless.

The reasons for homelessness are legion. After the two world wars, many homeless men were ex-soldiers who could not find work or just could not settle down; and this category remains. There are those discharged from prison with no home to go to; those who have suffered mental illness, with no family to take them in on being discharged from hospital; and those handicapped by other forms of illness or disability. Some have lost the jobs which previously supplied them with accommodation; and of course there will always be some who choose vagrancy as a way of life — but all are in need of help. By far the most numerous are those who suffer from alcoholism and drug addiction. The numbers of people suffering in this way have risen considerably in recent years, and among the homeless alcoholism and drug addiction are most prevalent as a means of temporarily forgetting their lot and in bad weather of affording some means of deadening the body to the cold.

Who are the homeless poor? Few people choose to become homeless. The old-fashioned tramp is almost extinct: most of those on the streets today are there through circumstances beyond their control. The young school-leaver who moves away from home to seek a better life in a big city may find only the corrupting culture of the street. The married man without work, humiliated by loss of his status in the family, despondently seeks oblivion in a strange town.

The institutionalised man, so often today a long-term psychiatric patient released without adequate after-care, wanders from hostel to hostel, isolated and increasingly anti-social. The petty criminal whom society rejects in an unforgiving way can hope, at most, for casual work. The old age pensioner, without family and out of touch with friends, cannot cope with the hopelessness of life without focus. Women also must be considered: young pregnant girls rejected by family, battered wives, psychiatric patients, and widows alone without friends.

In hard times, without faith or family to support them, a crisis can render a person homeless. This does not affect only certain classes. A company director who lost both his sons in a car accident on holiday from a public school was then faced with his wife's suicide. He took to the streets. With such could be included priests, barristers and other professional men who for one reason or another become unequal to life's demands. The Church has offered hospitality to all such people in the past. Today the state is unequal to the task without voluntary support; this gives Christians an added incentive to show their faith by their works (Jm 2:14–17).

Notes

[1] This chapter is taken, with minor alterations, from the author's *The Church's Response to the Homeless* (Great Wakering, McCrimmon, 1985), pp.11–15.

[2] For an overview of the whole area, see P. Slack, *Poverty and Policy in Tudor and Stuart England* (London and New York, Longman, 1988). For a recent account of the practical and theoretical issues with which Elizabethan parishes grappled, based partly on the records of the town of Hadleigh, see M. K. McIntosh, Poverty, Charity and Coercion in Elizabethan

England, in *The Journal of Interdisciplinary History*, vol. 35, no. 3 *Poverty and Charity: Judaism, Christianity and Islam* (Winter 2005), pp. 457–479.

3   For an account of Catholic attempts to deal with these problems, see B. Pullan, Catholics, Protestants and the Poor in Early Modern Europe, in *The Journal of Interdisciplinary History*, vol. 35, no. 3 *Poverty and Charity: Judaism, Christianity and Islam* (Winter 2005), pp. 441–456.

4   Quoted by E. P. Thompson in *The Making of the English Working Class*, new ed. (Harmondsworth, Penguin, 1968), p. 295.

CHAPTER 14

THE RE-AWAKENING OF CHRISTIAN SOCIAL CONSCIENCE IN ENGLAND[1]

THE VACUUM LEFT in care for the poor by the dissolution of the religious houses was partially filled in later years by dissenting Christian movements. With the reawakening of a Christian social conscience, the eighteenth and nineteenth centuries witnessed a number of such initiatives on behalf of the spiritual as well as the material needs of the poor.

The Methodists, founded by a Church of England clergyman, John Wesley, were one of these movements. They were known as Methodist because of their methodical approach to their religion, and took to preaching to the poor in the open air after the Church of England authorities banned many of them from their churches. Many poor took to Methodism, particularly in the west of Britain, where there had once been great resistance to the Reformation. The primitive Methodists had a special concern for the poor and by the middle of the nineteenth century the movement as a whole was leading the fight against injustice to the poor, building mission halls in large cities and launching social initiatives in the slum areas.

The Congregationalists also did much for the poor, especially aiding those who sought a new life in the colonies. The London Missionary Society, formed in 1795, originally non-denominational, became a Congregationalist institution. In 1831 this movement formed a union and campaigned on behalf of the poor, the abolition of slavery, and the repeal of the Corn Laws. Like the Methodists they were concerned for the education of poor children and built schools and trained teachers to staff them.

The Baptists were also very active among the underprivileged. One of the pioneers of what today is called social work was a Baptist called Robert Hall; and in 1792 the Baptist Missionary Society was formed to extend this work. These movements were labelled non-conformist by the establishment, but they did much pioneer work in restoring a Christian social conscience in Britain and in reviving the mission to the poor.

The Catholic Church's charitable work in Britain may compare unfavourably with her record in the early Middle Ages, but the confiscation of monastic and other church property at the Dissolution, and years of persecution, present a major obstacle from which full recovery has yet to be made. The French Revolution was ironically perhaps the first stage in the re-establishment of the Church's charitable work in Britain; the French revolutionary government's expulsion of religious orders in the 1790s caused a substantial exodus to Protestant Britain. Notable among the refugees were the Sisters of Charity, founded by St Vincent de Paul in 1633 in the wake of the counter-reformation. Other religious orders and charitable societies, such as the Little Sisters of the Poor, founded in 1854, and the Society of St Vincent de Paul, founded in 1833, were to follow, settling in Britain long after the revolution had given way to Napoleon. Added to these religious and charitable societies were the English Ladies (Institute of the Blessed Virgin) and the Sisters of the Good Shepherd, who with the other communities formed a substantial body which could give the Church's mission to the poor in Britain a new impetus.

Before the foundation of the Salvation Army in 1865 and of the Church Army (a voluntary Anglican organisation modelled on the former) in 1882, the Catholic mission to the poor and homeless had already made a considerable contribution. The Catholic shelter in Crispin Street, London, opened in 1860, taking 130 women and 150 men. It was described as clean and without religious discrimination. The nation's conscience had been awakened, moreover, by individual philanthropists such as Elizabeth Fry and John Howard in prison reform.

The Catholic social ethic was in part recovered by the high Anglican Tractarians at the turn of the century: they considered that revolution based on true doctrine was the only way to attack social problems. Dr Demant, Professor of Moral and Pastoral Theology at Oxford, although an Anglican, did much to recover Catholic social teaching and set the scene for a revival of religious action, but in many cases religious incentives succumbed to political expediency.

However, these charities came more and more under the control of the Government and thus laid the foundations of the welfare state. By 1942 state supervision of the nation's welfare had made enormous progress, and from this time it could be said that the welfare state was born. However, such control had its limitations, above all its lack of the personal touch; and over the years it proved more wasteful than private charity. Public relief funded by taxation can supplant appeals to individual conscience and undermine the spontaneity of personal responsibility to those in need.

It is not that state support should be discontinued; but it must not sap private initiative. State-sponsored charity has given rise to social work as a state-paid profession. Workers in this field are becoming increasingly aware of the value of the private charity, and in this Catholic charity should be foremost.

For all its achievements, the welfare state did detract from Christian initiative. With the coining of the term 'social work' in the 1950s, a new understanding developed in which Christian faith was no longer seen as the underlying motivation. The state-paid social worker took over many areas of human need, and politics frequently replaced religion (although, to be fair, the state took the initiative where Christians had suffered a massive loss of nerve).

State support of the poor through taxation has inevitably diminished the level of Christian charity. Political theory has in part discouraged voluntary charitable activity and materialistic theory has dissipated the altruism of Christian action. Possession of material well-being has been presented as the supreme good, irrespective of any Christian ends, and man can be seen to be served for himself and for his own satisfaction. These secularising and humanist tendencies have taken their toll of the Church's charitable works since the 1960s; priests and nuns have left their vocations to become social workers instead of directing their existing mission to the needy. Quite apart from the long-term effects of the Reformation, contemporary political, economic and social trends have severely hampered the Church's charitable works.

In recent years, however, the limitations and defects of state charity have become more apparent: the salaried worker with fixed hours of work cannot always satisfactorily replace the dedicated religious; sympathetic legislation, no matter how enlightened, cannot always equal the altruism of individual Christians. Private charities economise on administration and so can spend more money on their main purpose. Public relief, on the other hand, which can be claimed as of right, must perforce expend much revenue on administration. To be fair, however, the welfare state has done much to create a caring society and in recent years the legacy of the workhouse has been somewhat eradicated. Many private charities could not exist without government support, but on the other hand the state is unequal to the task of providing much of the care provided by private charities. This suggests a union of private initiative and public finance. Christian teaching provided the framework for such initiative in the past: indeed the Church was the first in the field and has met the needs of every age internationally, in proportion to her resources, more adequately and more continuously than any other agency.

Many now believe that the scope of private charities should be extended, and that Christian charities should occupy the foremost place and perform the largest and most effective work. The Decree of the Second Vatican Council on the Renewal of the Religious Life requires two simultaneous processes: (i) a continuous return to the source of all Christian life and to the original inspiration behind a given community, and (ii) an adjustment of the community to the changed conditions of the times. Many religious communities sprang up in answer to the needs of the poor, the sick, and the homeless, and the Council encourages a return to this inspiration.[2]

Among Catholic charities, Mother Teresa's Missionaries of Charity have set a marvellous example and taken a lead in setting up hostels for the poor in this country. Father James Fergusson has started a number of 'Jericho' houses in Scotland, catering for the homeless, alcoholics, battered wives, and others; and the Daughters of Charity have established a day centre at Westminster. The Society of St Dismas runs a hostel for ex-prisoners in Southampton; and the St Thomas Fund for the Homeless has recently opened hostels in Brighton, Hove, and Shoreham-by-Sea. These developments indicate a continuing revival of the Church's mission and its adaptation to the changing pattern of human need. The most consistent contribution continues to be that of the lay Society of St Vincent de Paul, who have provided a bridgehead between the pre-Reformation Church and the mission of today's church. All this gives special emphasis to the importance of the lay vocation, which has not infrequently outstripped many religious communities in Christian service to the poor and homeless.

Notes

[1] This chapter is taken, with minor alterations, from the author's *The Church's Response to the Homeless* (Great Wakering, McCrimmon, 1985), pp. 17–20.

[2] Vatican II, Decree on the Adaptation and Renewal of Religious Life *Perfectae Caritatis* (28 October 1965).

CHAPTER 15

THE ORDER OF MALTA AND THE RENAISSANCE OF HOSPITALLER WORK

THE HOSPITALLERS ESTABLISHED a new headquarters in Rome in 1834, but it was Pope Leo XIII's restoration of a Grand Master to the Order in 1879 that signalled the renaissance of the Order as a humanitarian and religious enterprise. Care of the poor and sick once more became a Hospitaller priority, particularly under Ludovico Chigi della Rovere Albani (Grand Master 1931–51), and was greatly expanded during the two world wars. The Order has recently returned to Malta, after signing an agreement with the Government, and now has the use of its old fort of St Angelo.

Under the title of The Sovereign Military Hospitaller Order of Jerusalem, Rhodes, and Malta, the Order acts as a virtual sovereign state with diplomatic status in many countries. Moreover today its Hospitaller ministry has extended worldwide, proving that its mission of hospitality has ensured not only its survival but also its global expansion. The Order of Malta, as the Order is commonly called, now has up to forty seven national associations, added to which there are six sub-priories and six grand priories.

Each of these national associations has the responsibility of caring for the sick and the poor in a number of ways. For instance in 1974 a former President of the

British Association proposed a joint venture to provide housing and care for the elderly with the Venerable Order of St John, an Order of Chivalry which was constituted by a Royal Charter of 1888 and has the reigning monarch of the United Kingdom as its Sovereign Head. A trust was established named the Order of Malta Homes Trust and the British Association launched an appeal, which raised the initial sum of £150,000. The first property was soon to follow. The then Chancellor of the British Association invited the author to lunch at his club to discuss a suitable property with which to commence the venture. The author suggested Arundel Priory, owned by the Duke of Norfolk and at that time unoccupied, consisting of a fine fourteenth century quadrangle abutting the chancel of the old parish church, which remained in the Duke's possession as the tomb house of his ancestors.

The Norfolk Estates decided to grant the Order of Malta Homes Trust a long lease on the Priory, a Grade I listed building in need of much restoration. Help and advice came from Servite Housing, a local Catholic charity which had had much experience in the conversion of old buildings, having just converted the Servite Priory at Bognor Regis to sheltered housing. The necessary funds to convert the Priory were obtained from the Housing Corporation, as it then was. The area in the quadrangle adjoining the chapel was converted into eight flats and a care home for the elderly. On the 18th of June 1981, the feast of Corpus Christi, the Priory was opened by Archbishop Bruno Heim, the Apostolic Delegate of Great Britain (the following year he became the first Pro-Nuncio since the Reformation).

At the same time the Trust was expanding into the field of almshouses and was appointed a trustee of almshouses in Ruthin and Llandwrog in North Wales. Almshouses in Stockport, Cheshire, Newcastle, and London followed, with a day centre at Newcastle. Then in 1991 the Trust contracted with Lincolnshire County Council to take over sixteen more care homes in the county. To run these care homes, the Orders of St John Care Trust was set up separate from the Order of Malta Homes Trust. This was a joint venture with the Venerable Order of St John, each having its own patron, under the chairmanship of a member of the Order of Malta. Since these homes were taken over in May 1992 this venture has expanded enormously.

The Orders of St John Care Trust is now the principal work of the British Association of the Sovereign Military Order of Malta in the United Kingdom. There are 73 care homes in Oxfordshire, Wiltshire, Gloucestershire, and Lincolnshire, with the original care home at Arundel. This requires 4,000 staff to care for 3,300 residents, including nursing and day care. There are also respite care facilities and care for those suffering from dementia and similar conditions. Moreover the Trust runs its own training scheme for the carers in its employ.

The priories of the Order of Malta incorporate, among others, those who have taken vows. Such members thus constitute a religious community as part of the protean nature of the Order. Many of the national associations are not limited by their own boundaries but provide support for relief work for other poorer countries, particularly in cases of natural disasters. The Order has an international fleet of thirty ambulance services providing first aid for those in need. Among these the Irish Association has an ambulance corps covering Southern Ireland and also trains staff for the Order's Maternity Hospital in Bethlehem. The Austrian Grand Priory has a first aid emergency service and distributes medicines to the Near East and Eastern Europe. The French and Belgian Associations do much to support the Order's Maternity Hospital in Bethlehem and run hospitals and care homes in many African countries as well as teaching first aid. In Switzerland the Order has an international body that cares for lepers in South East Asia and South America and the North American Associations support the poor in the Caribbean and in central and South America.[1]

The Order also has a relief organization called Malteser International which reaches out to worldwide needs providing relief and reconstruction and is supported by many of the national associations. The aid, like the first hospital of St John in Jerusalem, is provided without favour to race, religion, or politics, firmly based on Gospel values. Malteser International, together with other international aid agencies, gave assistance to the victims of the Indian Ocean tsunami in 2004, the cyclone in Burma of 2008, and the earthquake which struck Haiti in 2010. The Order was the first into Haiti and has had a major share in the support and reconstruction programme. It does not just provide initial help but also provides long stay support for future development and education in disaster remedies and prevention.[2]

In the countries where the Order of Malta operates it runs health care programmes including nutrition advice, hygiene, sanitation, and advice on the provision of drinking water. In 1992 the Order set up the Emergency Corps of the Order of Malta to better coordinate all the activities of the national associations until the merger of the various agencies into Malteser

International. Aid agencies like the Order of Malta have to respond not only to natural disasters but also to the human crises caused by war, revolution, and the famine that these conditions often create. One of these areas is the Democratic Republic of Congo which is engulfed in armed conflict. Many have been forced to flee in fear of their lives as violence, hunger and disease stalk their villages. Malteser International has been working here since the mid 1990s and at present has 135 national and eight international staff members giving support. In 2008 and 2009 these staff members provided thousands of tons of food, including flour, vegetables, oil and salt. They also contributed a trauma clinic to support the victims of violence, providing a truly compassionate support in the finest Hospitaller tradition.[3]

Despite the nature of these disaster areas, they only represent some 10% of Malteser International's worldwide ministry. Malteser International's greatest focus is on eastern Africa, India, parts of Asia, and South America. In these places it provides medicine, clinics, surgeries as well as clean water programmes, sewage treatment and home improvements. There are also health programmes with provision of vaccination. Other practical provisions include rainwater harvesting tanks, eco-friendly sewage plants, and lavatories. Programmes to counter HIV/Aids, leprosy, and tuberculosis are also found at the heart of Malteser International's ministry.[4]

Thus since the eleventh century the Order can boast of a continuous ministry of care second to none as one of the world's most effective aid agencies with 13,000 members, 80,000 permanent volunteers and 20,000 medical staff. The Order reaches out to the sick, the poor, the elderly, the handicapped, the refugees, the homeless and the lepers, without distinction of race or religion in every corner of the world. Thus it could be said that the Hospitaller vocation, in practical terms, down the centuries, has proved to be the greatest benefit to humanity. The Order of Malta, as the oldest order of chivalry, has risen above what might have been a self-indulgent anachronism of old world pageantry, to provide a truly international and efficient service to the sick and the poor. As a religious order, unlike most, it has truly embraced the spirit of its founder and has extended its ministry of mercy to global proportions.

In fine, the words of Pope Benedict XVI remind us of the Order's high aspiration.

> Dear Knights of the Sovereign Military Order of Malta, dear doctors, nurses and all who work here, you are all called to carry out an important service to the sick and to society, a service that demands self-denial and a spirit of sacrifice. In every sick person, whoever he or she may be, may you be able to recognize and serve Christ himself; make them perceive with your acts and words the signs of his merciful love.[5]

The Church should be justly proud of a mission to the sick and the poor which now spans nine hundred years and has kept alive our Lord's admonition, 'As you did it to one of the least of these my brethren, you did it to me' (Mt 25:40).

Notes

[1] V. Horsler, P. Leslie & J. Andrews, *The Order of Malta, A Portrait* (London, Third Millennium Publishing, 2011), p. 139.

2   *Ibid.,* pp. 139–140.
3   *Ibid.,* pp. 140–143.
4   *Ibid.,* pp. 148–149.
5   Pope Benedict XVI, *Address given at St John the Baptist Roman Hospital of the Sovereign Military Hospitaller Order of Malta* (2 December 2007).

APPENDIX

Address of His Holiness Pope Benedict XVI to the Order of Malta on 9 February 2013

Dear Brothers and Sisters!
    I am happy to welcome and to greet each one of you, Knights and Dames, chaplains and volunteers, of the Sovereign Military Order of Malta. I greet in a special way the Grand Master, His Most Eminent Highness Fra' Matthew Festing, and I thank him for his kind words addressed to me in the name of all of you; I also thank you for the gift you wished to offer me, which I will dedicate to a work of charity. My affectionate thoughts go to the Cardinals and to my brother bishops and priests, in particular to my Secretary of State, who has just presided at the Eucharist, and to Cardinal Paolo Sardi, Patron of the Order, whom I thank for the care with which he strives to strengthen the special bond that joins you to the Catholic Church and most particularly to the Holy See. With gratitude, I greet Archbishop Angelo Acerbi, your Prelate. A final word of greeting goes to the diplomats and to all the high dignitaries and authorities who are present.
    The occasion that brings us together is the ninth centenary of the solemn privilege *Pie Postulatio Voluntatis* of 15 February 1113, by which Pope Paschal II placed the newly created 'hospitaller fraternity' of Jerusalem, dedicated to Saint John the Baptist, under the protection of the Church, and gave it sovereign

status, constituting it as an Order in church law, with the faculty freely to elect its superiors without interference from other lay or religious authorities. This important event takes on a special meaning in the context of the Year of Faith, during which the Church is called to renew the joy and the commitment of believing in Jesus Christ, the one Saviour of the world. In this regard, you too are called to welcome this time of grace, so as to deepen your knowledge of the Lord and to cause the truth and beauty of the faith to shine forth, through the witness of your lives and your service, in this present time.

Your Order, from its earliest days, has been marked by fidelity to the Church and to the Successor of Peter, and also for its unrenounceable spiritual identity, characterized by high religious ideals. Continue to walk along this path, bearing concrete witness to the transforming power of faith. By faith the Apostles left everything to follow Jesus, and then went out to the whole world, in fulfilment of his command to bring the Gospel to every creature; fearlessly they proclaimed to all people the power of the cross and the joy of the resurrection of Christ, which they had witnessed directly. By faith, the martyrs gave their lives, demonstrating the truth of the Gospel which had transformed them and made them capable of attaining to the highest gift, the fruit of love: that of forgiving their persecutors. And by faith, down the centuries, the members of your Order have given themselves completely, firstly in the care of the sick in Jerusalem and then in aid to pilgrims in the Holy Land who were exposed to grave dangers: their lives have added radiant pages to the annals of Christian charity and protection of Christianity. In the nineteenth century, the Order opened up to new and more ample forms of apostolate in the area of charitable assistance and service of the sick and the poor, but without ever abandoning the original ideals, especially that of the intense spiritual life of individual members. In this sense, your commitment must continue with a very particular attention to the religious consecration—of the professed members—which constitutes the heart of the Order. You must never forget your roots, when Blessed Gérard and his companions consecrated themselves with vows to the service of the poor, and their vocation was sanctioned by the privilege *Pie Postulatio Voluntatis*. The members of the newly created institute were thus configured with the features of religious life: commitment to attain Christian perfection by profession of the three vows, the charism for which they were consecrated, and fraternity among the members. The vocation of the professed members, still today, must be the object of great attention, combined with attention to the spiritual life of all.

In this sense, your Order, compared with other organizations that are committed in the international arena to the care of the sick, to solidarity and to human promotion, is distinguished by the Christian inspiration that must constantly direct the social engagement of its members. Be sure to preserve and cultivate this your qualifying characteristic and work with renewed apostolic ardour, maintaining an attitude of profound harmony with the Magisterium of the Church. Your esteemed and beneficent activity, carried out in a variety of fields and in different parts of the world, and particularly focused on care of the sick through hospitals and health-care institutes, is not mere philanthropy, but an effective expression and a living testimony of evangelical love.

In Sacred Scripture, the summons to love of neighbour is tied to the commandment to love God with all our heart, all our soul and all our strength (cf. Mk 12:29–31). Thus, love of neighbour—if based on a true love for God—corresponds to the commandment and the example of Christ. It is possible, then, for the Christian, through his or her dedication, to bring others to experience the bountiful tenderness of our heavenly Father, through an ever deeper conformation to Christ. In order to offer love to our brothers and sisters, we must be afire with it from the furnace of divine charity: through prayer, constant listening to the word of God, and a life centred on the Eucharist. Your daily life must be imbued with the presence of Jesus, under whose gaze you are called to place the sufferings of the sick, the loneliness of the elderly, the difficulties of the disabled. In reaching out to these people, you are serving Christ: 'as you did it to one of the least of these my brethren, you did it to me' (Mt 25:40).

Dear friends, continue working in society and in the world along the elevated paths indicated by the Gospel—faith and charity, for the renewal of hope: faith, as testimony of adherence to Christ and of commitment to the Gospel mission, which inspires you to an ever more vital presence in the ecclesial community and to an ever more conscious membership of the people of God; charity, as an expression of fraternity in Christ, through works of mercy for the sick, the poor, those in need of love, comfort and assistance, those who are afflicted by loneliness, by a sense of bewilderment and by new material and spiritual forms of poverty. These ideals are aptly expressed in your motto: '*Tuitio fidei et obsequium pauperum.*' These words summarize well the charism of your Order which, as a subject of international law, aims not to exercise power and influence of a worldly character, but in complete freedom to accomplish its own mission for the integral good of man, spirit and body, both individually and collectively, with special regard to those whose need of hope and love is greater.

May the Holy Virgin, Our Lady of Philermos, support your plans and projects with her maternal protection; may your heavenly protector Saint John the Baptist and Blessed Gérard, as well as the saints and blesseds of the Order, accompany you with their intercession. For my part, I promise to pray for all those present here, for all the members of the Order, as well as the numerous worthy volunteers, including a significant number of children, and for all who work alongside you. Affectionately, I impart to you a special Apostolic Blessing, which I willingly extend to your families.

BIBLIOGRAPHY

Biblical Texts

The Bible, Revised Standard Edition, Old Testament (1951) and New Testament, 2nd ed. (1971)

Primary Sources

Life of Aelred, in *The Life of Aelred of Rievaulx by Walter Daniel*, trans. from the Latin and annotated by F. M. Powicke, introduction by M. Dutton (Kalamazoo, Michigan, Cistercian Publications, 1994)

Aristides, *Apology*, in *The Apology of Aristides*, trans W. S. Walford (London, 1909)

The Rule of St Benedict in English, ed. T. Fry (Collegeville, Minnesota, The Liturgical Press, 1982)

Brinklow, H., in *Henry Brinklow's Complaynt of Roderyck Mors sometyme a gray fryre unto the parliament howse of England ...(about A.D. 1542) and The Lamentacyon of a Christian agaynst the Cytye of London*, ed. J. M. Cowper (London, Early English Text Society, extra ser., 22, 1874)

Brinklow, H., in *A Supplicacyon for the beggers, with A supplycacion to our moste soveraigne lord Kynge Henry the Eyght, A supplication of the poore commons, ...* ed. J. M. Cowper (London, Early English Text Society, extra ser., 18, 1871)

St Clement, *Epistles*, in *The Epistles of St Clement of Rome and St Ignatius of Antioch*, trans. J. A. Kleist (Westminster, Maryland, Newman Press, London, Longmans Green, 1946)

St Cyprian of Carthage, *Letters*, in *The Writings of Cyprian, Bishop of Carthage*, trans. R. E. Wallis, vol. 1 (Edinburgh, T. & T. Clark, 1868)

St Cyprian of Carthage, *Work and Alms*, in *St Cyprian: Treatises*, trans. and ed. by R. J. Deferrari (Washington, Catholic University of America Press, 1981)

The Desert Fathers, trans. from the Latin with an introduction by H. Waddell (Constable & Co Ltd, 1936)

Didascalia Apostolorum, the Syriac Version trans. and accompanied by the Verona Latin Fragments with an intro. and notes by R. H. Connolly (Oxford, The Clarendon Press, 1929)

Eusebius, *Ecclesiastical History*, in *Eusebius: Church History, Life of Constantine the Great etc.* trans. by A. C. McGiffert and others. (Oxford, 1890)

Fowler, J. T., *The Rites of Durham, being a description or brief declaration of all the ancient monuments, rites and customs belonging or being within the monastical church of Durham before the suppression, written 1593*, ed. J. T. Fowler (Durham, Surtees Society, vol. cvii, 1902)

St Francis, in *Opuscula Sancti Francisci*, ed. PP. Collegii Sancti Bonaventurae (Florence, Quaracchi, 1904)

John of Würzburg, Descriptio Terrae Sanctae, ed. T. Tobler, in *Descriptiones terrae Sanctae ex saeculo VIII, IX, XII & XV* (Leipzig, 1874)

St Justin Martyr, *Apology*, in *The First Apology, the Second Apology, the Dialogue with Trypho, Exhortations to the Greeks, Discourse to the Greeks, the Monarchy or the Rule of God, by St Justin Martyr*, trans. T. B. Falls (Washington, Catholic University of America Press, 1977)

Lanfranc, *Monastic Constitutions*, in *The Monastic Constitutions of Lanfranc*, ed. D. Knowles, rev. C. N. L. Brooke (Oxford, Oxford University Press, 2002)

Liber Pontificalis of Edmund Lacy, Bishop of Exeter, ed. R. Barnes (Exeter, William Roberts, 1847)

Matthew Paris, Chronica Majora, in *Matthaei Parisiensis Monachi Sancti Albani Chronica Majora* ed. H. R. Luard (London, Longman, 1872–83)

Possidius, *Life of St Augustine*, in *Sancti Augustini Vita Scripta a Possidio Episcope*, ed. H. T. Weiskotten (Nabu Press, 2010)

Tertullian, *Apology*, in *Q. Septimi Florentis Tertulliani Apologeticus*, trans. A. Souter, ed. F. Oehler and J. E. B. Mayor (Cambridge, Cambridge University Press, 2011)

William of Tyre, *Historia Rerum in Partibus Transmarinis Gestarum*, in *A History of Deeds Done Beyond the Sea, by William of Tyre*, trans. E. A. Babcock and A. Krey, 2 vols. (New York, Columbia University Press, 1944)

Decree on the Adaptation and Renewal of the Religious Life Perfectae Caritatis, proclaimed by his Holiness Pope Paul VI, on October 28, 1965

Secondary Sources

Ashley, W. J., *An Introduction to English Economic History and Theory*, 4th ed. (London, Longmans Green, 1906), 2 vols.

Barclay, W., *The Plain Man Looks at the Beatitudes* (London, Fontana, 1965)

Balthasar, H. U. von, *The Office of Peter and the Structure of the Church*, 2nd ed., trans A. Emery (San Francisco, Ignatius, 1986)

Baskerville, G., *The English Monks and the Suppression of the Monasteries* (London, Jonathan Cape, 1937)

Bird, F. B., A Comparative Study of the Work of Charity in Christianity and Judaism, in *The Journal of Religious Ethics*, vol. 10, no. 1 (Spring 1982), pp. 144–69

Brown, P., *Augustine of Hippo: a Biography* (London, Faber and Faber, 1967)

Burke, S. H., *Historical Portraits of the Tudor Dynasty and the Reformation Period*, (London, John Hodges, 1879–83), 4 vols.

Canavan, J. E., Charity in the Early Church, in *Studies: An Irish Quarterly Review*, vol. 12, no. 45 (March 1923), pp. 61–77

Cohen, M. R., *Poverty and Charity in the Jewish Community of Medieval Egypt* (Princeton and Oxford, Princeton University Press, 2005)

Clay, R. M., *The Mediaeval Hospitals of England* (London, Methuen & Co., 1909)

Daniel-Rops, H., *The Church of Apostles and Martyrs*, trans. A. Butler (London & New York, J. M. Dent & Sons Ltd & E. P. Dutton & Co. Inc., 1960)

Duchesne, L., *Early History of the Christian Church from its Foundation to the End of the Fifth Century*, trans. from the 4th ed., 3 vols. (London, John Murray, 1909–24)

Eliot, T. S., *The Idea of a Christian Society* (London, Faber & Faber, 1939)

Ehrle, F., *Beiträge zur Geschichte und Reform der Armenpflege* (Freiburg, 1881)

Elvins, M. T., *The Church's Response to the Homeless* (Great Wakering, Essex, Mayhew McCrimmon, 1985)

Frend, W. H. C., *The Early Church* (London, Hodder and Stoughton, 1965)

Friedlander, G., *The Jewish Sources for the Sermon on the Mount* (London, George Routledge & Sons Ltd, 1911)

Gasquet, F. A., *English Monastic Life* (London, Methuen and Co, 1904)

Gasquet, F. A., *Parish Life in Mediaeval England*, 6th ed. (London, Methuen, 1929)

Hands, A. R., *Charities and Social Aid in Greece and Rome* (London, Thames and Hudson, 1968).

Heal, F., *Hospitality in Early Modern England* (Oxford, Clarendon Press, 1990)

Hordern, P., The Earliest Hospitals in Byzantium, Western Europe, and Islam, in *The Journal of Interdisciplinary History*, vol. 35, no. 3 *Poverty and Charity: Judaism, Christianity and Islam* (Winter 2005), pp. 361–389

Horsler, V., with Leslie, P., *The Order of Malta: a Portrait* (London, Third Millenium Publishing, 2011)

Kent, G., *Poverty* (London, Batsford, 1968)

King, E. J., *The Rule Statutes and Customs of the Hospitallers, 1099–1310* (London, Methuen & Co, 1934)

Knowles, D., *The Religious Orders in England*, 3 vols. (Cambridge, Cambridge University Press, 1948–59)

Kottek, S. S. The Hospital in Jewish History, in *Reviews of Infectious Diseases*, vol. 3, no. 4, *Nosocomial Infection Control* (Jul.–Aug. 1981), pp. 636–9

Lallemand, L., *Histoire de la Charité*, 4 vols. (Paris, 1902–12)

Lambert, M. D., *Franciscan Poverty: The Doctrine of the Absolute Poverty of Christ and the Apostles in the Franciscan Order, 1210–1323*, rev. and expanded ed. (New York, Franciscan Institute, 1998)

Lecky, W., *A History of European Morals from Augustus to Charlemagne* (New York & London, D. Appleton and Co, 1921)

Mark of Whitstable (pseudonym for Elvins, M. T.), *Gospel Chivalry: Franciscan Romanticism* (Leominster, Gracewing Publishing, 2006)

McIntosh, M. K., Poverty, Charity and Coercion in Elizabethan England, in *The Journal of Interdisciplinary History*, vol. 35, no. 3 *Poverty and Charity: Judaism, Christianity and Islam* (Winter 2005), pp. 457–79.

Miller, T. S., The Knights of St John and the Hospital of the Latin West, in *Speculum*, vol. 53, no. 4 (Oct. 1978), pp. 709–33

Mollat, M., *The Poor in the Middle Ages: An Essay in Social History*, trans. from the French by A. Goldhammer (New Haven and London, Yale University Press, 1986)

Moorman, J. R. H., *Church Life in England in the Thirteenth Century* (Cambridge, Cambridge University Press, 1945)

Nicholson, H. J., *The Knights Hospitaller* (Woodbridge, Boydell Press, 2001)

Phan, P. C., *Social Thought* (Wilmington, Delaware, M. Glazier Inc., 1984)

Pashley, R., *Pauperism and Poor Laws* (London, Longman Brown Green and Longmans, 1852)

Pullan, B., Catholics, Protestants and the Poor in Early Modern Europe, in *The Journal of Interdisciplinary History*, vol. 35, no. 3 *Poverty and Charity: Judaism, Christianity and Islam* (Winter 2005), pp. 441–456

Ratzinger, G., *Der Geschichte Kirchlichen Armenpflege* (Freiburg, Freiburg Univ., 1884)

Riley-Smith, J. S. C., *A History of the Order of the Hospital of St John in Jerusalem*, vol. 1: *The Knights of St John in Jerusalem and Cyprus, c. 1050–1310* (London and New York, MacMillan, St Martin's Press, 1967)

Scarisbrick, J. J., *The Reformation and the English People* (Oxford, Basil Blackwell, 1984)

Sire, H. J. A., *The Knights of Malta* (New Haven and London, Yale University Press, 1994)

Slack, P., *Poverty and Policy in Tudor and Stuart England* (London and New York, Longman, 1988)

Thompson, E. P., *The Making of the English Working Class*, new ed. (Harmondsworth, Penguin, 1968)

Tierney, B., *Medieval Poor Law: A Sketch of Canonical Theory and its Appreciation in England* (Berkeley and Los Angeles, University of California Press, 1959)

Troeltsch, E., *The Social Teaching of the Christian Churches*, with an introduction by H. R. Niebuhr, trans. O. Wyon, 2 vols. (Chicago and London, University of Chicago Press, 1981)

Uhlhorn, J. G. W., *Christian Charity in the Ancient Church* (New York, C. Scribner's Sons, 1881)

Walsh, J. J., *The Catholic Church and Healing* (London, Burns Oates and Washbourne Ltd, 1928)

Woodward, J. H., *To Do the Sick No Harm: a Study of the British Voluntary Hospital System to 1875* (London and Boston, Massachusetts, Routledge and Kegan Paul, 1974)

www.ingramcontent.com/pod-product-compliance
Lightning Source LLC
Chambersburg PA
CBHW032257150426
43195CB00008BA/487